The Power
of
Faith and Prayer

The Power
of
Faith and Prayer

SAMUEL RUTHERFORD

REFORMATION PRESS
2023

Published by
Reformation Press, 11 Churchill Drive, Stornoway
Isle of Lewis, Scotland HS1 2NP

www.reformationpress.co.uk

Originally published in 1713 as *The Power and Prevalency of Faith and Prayer
evidenced in a practical discourse upon Matth. 9. 27–31*

Published by Reformation Press as: *The Power of Faith and Prayer*
1st edition: 1991
2nd edition: 2023

The present edition is edited and annotated by Dr R.J. Dickie
Cover photograph: Douglas McGilviray
Cover design by A4 Design and Print
Revised and repunctuated text, layout and additional material are
© Reformation Press 1991 and 2023

Paperback printed by www.lulu.com

British Library Cataloguing-in-Publication Data
A catalogue record for this book is available
from the British Library

ISBN numbers
Paperback: 978-1-872556-58-1
E-book: 978-1-4466-9576-0

All rights reserved. No part of this publication may be reproduced,
stored in a retrieval system, or transmitted, in any form or by any
means, without the prior permission in writing of Reformation Press,
or as expressly permitted by law, by licence, or under terms agreed with
the appropriate reprographic rights organisation.

Contents

Publisher's preface.. 7

Foreword 11

Epistle to the Reader... 15

Introduction 23

Chapter 1   The occasion, or time, when Christ departed.... 25

Chapter 2   The subject of the miracle—two blind men...... 29

Chapter 3   The behaviour of the blind men........................ 32

Chapter 4   The qualification Christ requires of them.......... 58

Chapter 5   The blind men's confession of their faith.......... 75

Chapter 6   The cure 91

Publisher's preface

SAMUEL RUTHERFORD needs no introduction. He was probably the greatest theologian of the Scottish 'Second Reformation' period. His name is renowned the world over as the writer of many spiritual and devotional works. His letters were first published in 1662, and remain in print today, widely appreciated for their spiritual counsel. In *Scottish Theology in Relation to Church History since the Reformation*, Principal John Macleod described Rutherford's letters as 'the most remarkable series of devotional letters that the literature of the Reformed Churches can show. They are a religious classic which finds its warmest welcome where zeal for God's glory and love to the Lord Jesus Christ are a most vehement flame.'

The present book is one of the posthumous works of Rutherford. It was published in 1713, more than fifty years after his death in 1661. The slim volume was then entitled *The power and prevalency of faith and prayer evidenced in a practical discourse upon Matth. 9.27–31*, and the work ends abruptly in the incomplete sixth chapter, with the endpaper declaring, 'The rest of this discourse cannot be found, it being above 50 years since the author died.'

Despite being an incomplete work, the book provides a great insight into Rutherford's views of deep matters relating to the very life of the child of God. As well as dealing tenderly with the concerns of God's people regarding these subjects, Rutherford touches on several theological controversies which affected the Church in his day. These aspects of the book are just as relevant now as when he penned them well over three centuries ago.

Reformation Press issued this book in 1991, retitled more succinctly as *The Power of Faith and Prayer*. This was the first time the book had been reissued since its first appearance in 1713. The book was widely appreciated by people who love the writings of Samuel Rutherford.

Matthew Vogan, a recognised present-day expert on Rutherford, has now identified the context in which this book was written, and his findings have been published as 'Rutherford's *The Power and Prevalency of Prayer* and its Context' in volume 13 of the *Scottish Reformation Society Historical Journal* (2023), pp. 27–38). The publisher is very grateful to Matthew Vogan for summarising the background in his instructive Preface to this new edition of *The Power of Faith and Prayer*.

Rutherford had his own characteristic style of writing, incorporating Scots and Latin words without explanation or translation. Due to semantic drift the meanings of some English words have changed with the passage of the centuries, and other words have become obsolete. In order to preserve the original character of the book, the first *Reformation Press* edition (1993) supplied modern equivalents and explanations in brackets and footnotes. This second edition of *The Power of Faith and Prayer* furnishes a number of extra explanations, derived from standard reference works such as the *Oxford English Dictionary* and the *Dictionary of the Scots Language* (www.dsl.ac.uk), and punctuation of the text has now been updated to present-day conventions.

Those who love the writings of Samuel Rutherford will value this book—not simply as the reprint of an extremely scarce antiquarian book, but principally as an able treatise on the great matters of faith and prayer.

Publisher's Preface

In issuing this second edition of *The Power of Faith and Prayer*, it is the desire of the publisher that this book may be profitable to all who read it.

The Publisher, Stornoway
November 2023

Foreword

TWO RUTHERFORD SCHOLARS of the early twentieth century, James D. Ogilvie and William M. Campbell, believed that this book was one of the best literary productions from Rutherford's pen. It has its place along with the spiritual force of *The Trial and Triumph of Faith* (1645) and the exalted heights of Christ *Dying and Drawing Sinners to Himself* (1647). It also shares many of the themes of those volumes.

The Power of Faith and Prayer is a continued expository discourse on Matthew 9:27–31, which records the healing of two blind men who followed Christ, calling upon him. Presumably it derived from a series of sermons but the divisions between sermons are not explicitly marked. The incident is like the woman of Canaan passages brought out in *Trial and Triumph* in the way Christ is addressed as Son of David and in the cry made. It is no surprise therefore that Rutherford alludes to this account in the exposition on Matthew 9.

Some of the shared key themes in these volumes are the two natures of Christ, the nature of faith and prayer as well as assurance. The mutual dependence of faith and prayer are for instance brought out in a vivid and concise way in *The Power of Faith and Prayer*. 'Faith is often with child of prayer, and prayer with child of faith.' It is 'a circular generation', 'as when water putteth forth ice, and again ice produceth water; and vapours gender clouds and rain, and clouds and rain gender vapours'. We cannot 'separate praying and believing: praying without faith

11

is breathing of wind, and sounds without life'. Another key theme that is shared by all three volumes is the presence and absence of Christ in the communion that the believer experiences with him. These are what Rutherford calls 'the variations, the ebbings and flowings of God: this you may read in Solomon's Song, especially Chapter 3 and Chapter 5'.

While it shares these themes, there are in *The Power of Faith and Prayer* fewer digressions opposing the views of Antinomian and other writers compared with the two longer volumes. Thus the reader gains something of those books distilled in this slim treatise. No doubt it was for these reasons that James Ogilvie was ready to say, 'I believe this Discourse to be the finest thing which Rutherfurd ever wrote and one of the gems of Scottish devotional literature.'

The Power of Faith and Prayer not only shares the themes of those books, it was evidently preached during the same time period: Rutherford's years in London whilst attending the Westminster Assembly. Rutherford's reference to the civil sword and the sword of the stranger allows us to date it to the period following the campaigns of the Marquis of Montrose and his Irish troops in 1645. During that year and the years following the 'pestilence' or plague Rutherford also refers to was also at its height. It seems therefore that we can date these sermons to the end of 1645 or early 1646.

The present book was first published in Edinburgh in February 1713, with a long introduction by Rev. Allan Logan (died 1733), minister of Torryburn in Fife and later of Culross. Included with the treatise was the first publication of *A Testimony left by Mr Rutherfurd to the Work of Reformation in Britain and Ireland before his Death, with some of his last words*. It appears that Logan received the manuscript from the granddaughters of Samuel Rutherford through his daughter Agnes (the only child who survived him). The manuscript does not survive. It is not clear at what point Rutherford was preparing this treatise for

Foreword

publication but either the task was unfinished or the latter part of the treatise was lost. Logan says that the remaining part cannot be found, which leaves that question unresolved.

In the 'Epistle to the Reader' Logan seems intent both to produce something as long as the treatise itself and to insert abundant doctrinal polemic. He appreciates the clarity of doctrinal articulation in Rutherford's brief exposition and particularly emphasises 'the oneness of Christ's person' (i.e., divine and human natures), justification by faith alone, and faith as an instrumental but not meritorious condition of the covenant of grace. These were matters of controversy at the time. He also notes that Rutherford is against separation from the Church without justification. As a contemporary of later Covenanters like James Fraser of Brea, Logan alludes to the Cameronian dissenters from the Revolution Church settlement in this regard.

As Ogilvie indicates, there is a unique depth of spiritual experience in this brief work. Rutherford enters into the profundity of spiritual prayer in passages such as the following:

> There may be much praying where there is no crying. In some prayers, there is much tongue, little spirit and life; so, in some others there is much spirit, little tongue. Light sorrow will speak; extreme grief is dumb and cannot command one word. The deepest floods in their motion speak least, and slide down their banks without noise; shallow brooks flow with great tumbling and din. Some desires are above words, and come out in nothing but in sad sighs and deep groans (Romans 8:26–27).

Just as in *The Trial and Triumph of Faith,* Rutherford deals with the nature of apparently unanswered prayer in a careful pastoral manner. 'And the woman of Canaan saw no means, but much anger, wrath, sad refusals and heavy reproaches; yet she still believes and prescribes nothing to Christ.'

There is a solid doctrinal foundation to these sermons that is presented in warm and appealing language. Rutherford does not just starkly state sovereign and irresistible grace in a propositional way. He combines Scriptural and visual language to make a more powerfully vivid persuasive argument.

> Electing grace—justifying grace—is no changeling, nor a moon to grow or decrease, nor a sea to ebb or flow. Nor is Christ a changeling. He perfects the good work that he begins. He is the author and finisher of our faith.

As we might expect from his letters, Rutherford exalts Christ in the most attractive of ways. His two natures and mediatorial glory are opened up with evident delight.

> The Son of Man is the new Lord of the new paradise, who has handselled [purchased] heaven with our flesh, and heaven in him is our freehold [permanent possession]. Christ is the sinner's Magna Carta—his new patent, and his flesh is the new Broad Seal, his gospel the new charter.

'He went about doing good' is the prompt for new adoring views of the Redeemer. Christ as the Mediator, says Rutherford, is like a mighty river of life, brim-full of grace for sinners.

> Though Christ did good freely and deliberately, yet goodness and grace were in Christ—as with nature, he could not choose but do good. Grace was in him as a river; he could not keep it within the banks, it must flow over to needy sinners. It's as kindly [natural] to grace in Christ to vent itself for the good of sinners as for the floods to move and run and the fire to cast heat.

Here are but a few of the spiritually rich and powerful passages that can be encountered this discourse. There are many more to uncover on each page and you will need to discover and treasure them for yourself. May the Lord richly bless them to you.

Matthew Vogan, Inverness

Epistle to the Reader

Extracts from the 1713 edition

THE AUTHOR of this discourse was famous for piety as well as learning. Few in these latter ages knew more of the mystery of godliness, or were better acquainted with its life and power. He was a great student in that which is the sweetest and sublimest of all sciences, the knowledge of God and of his Son Christ Jesus (John 17:3). He searched the Scriptures and laboured, under the Spirit's conduct, to take up the mind of God therein. Neither did he sist [stop] in bare speculations of divine Truth, he made it his work to do God's will. He was religious in earnest. Living to God and acting for his glory was the business of his life. Thus he was confirmed that the doctrine was of God (John 7:17) and became a great proficient in the noblest of all arts, the art of pleasing God (Hebrews 11:5; 1 John 3:22).

He had many qualities that deserve imitation.

1. He was sound in the faith. He subjected his mind and judgement to the written Word, studied to be of one mind in everything with the Spirit of God who speaks therein, and was careful to teach nothing but what Christ had commanded (Matthew 28:20). It will be the care of every wise scribe and every faithful steward of divine mysteries, to know nothing in divinity beside what is written. There is safety in this, as well as wisdom (Deuteronomy 4:2, 12:32; Proverbs 30:6) to have

our theology a transcript of that in the Deity, which is the first, truest and purest divinity, the original and standard of all divine knowledge in men and angels (as far as God is pleased to reveal it). I shall not say our author was mistaken in nothing, but I may safely say his mistakes are few and he never affected to recede from the common doctrine of the Reformed Churches. They have an ill taste, who are most fond of new and strange opinions in religion.

2. He was a man of stability, his word of doctrine was not yea and nay. The changes in his time made no change in principles. The times were indeed trying and the alterations astonishing that fell out then in the civil state of Britain, all things being unhinged and turned upside down by the art and cunning of some self-seeking men who over-reached [outwitted] such as were upright and designed honest things.

3. He was a firm asserter of every part of our Reformation— in doctrine, discipline, worship, and government: all the truths and institutions of Christ were precious unto him. Nor did he fail to witness against opposite corruptions with a becoming zeal. In this respect he has given a fair example to all posterity. I hope it will be the endeavour of some in this Church to follow him in this. The truth of doctrine, the purity of worship and gospel ordinances are important things, and to declare and maintain these is perhaps one of the best offices men can do to the world.

4. He still maintained the obligation of our Covenants. He never varied in this matter—no, not when they were violated by a faction in England in the sight of the sun, and our land was invaded and made a field of blood for adhering to them by the men that had sworn them.

5. He was zealous for the power of religion. None pressed practical godliness at that time with greater vigour and success. That which is too true of many could not be said of him, that

Epistle to the Reader

zeal for lesser things had lessened his regard to the advantage of truth, piety, holiness, and the power of Christianity. No! To honour God and do good to men's souls was his great design and most upon his heart.

6. He was a true patriot, faithful to the interest and privileges of his country. He asserted the just rights, power, and greatness of our native Protestant princes, but still in a consistency with the safety of our religion and civil rights and privileges. He did not think that our kings were above the laws, had no limits set to their power, but might do to and with their subjects what they thought fit. The indefeasible right[1] of kings, their absolute power, with the unconditioned allegiance and subjection of the people, are things he could never understand or reconcile with the Word of God, the light of nature and the fundamental constitution of the Scottish and English monarchies.

He was a man of true Revolution principles,[2] a friend to humane and Christian liberty—and for owning these principles, our Prelatists had him under process [legal summons] and, had he lived a few weeks longer, they would have made him seal with his blood what he wrote with his pen.

7. He was a man of candour and integrity. His walk was in simplicity and godly sincerity. For this and other qualities, he was had in veneration by many of the opposite persuasion. And when he was under process, some of them were unwilling to meddle with him. A great Tory[3] said openly at that time, 'Let Mr. Rutherford alone, he will get heaven upon us all.' Nor was it a wonder that such as knew him had a value for him and were unwilling to take his blood on their heads. A divine much

---

[1] The right which cannot be forfeited or annulled.

[2] The principles which led to the expulsion of James II of England in 1688.

[3] A member of the party that opposed the exclusion of James II.

esteemed by most Prelatists in Scotland gave him a high character in my hearing: 'He was', said he, 'the most serious, pious, grave and devout man that ever I saw.' As the giver of this character had lived long and read much, so he had been acquainted with many of different persuasions.

❊ ❊ ❊

As the author was mighty in the Scriptures and skilful in the word of righteousness, so his way of writing has a relish of heaven. For:

1. It is evangelical. As Erasmus said of Luther, so say I of him, there is something apostolic in his writings.

2. He is often short and sententious, and says much in little.

3. He is plain and easy, especially in this discourse. In his controversial writings, he is sometimes more obscure to ordinary readers. Yet, when he falls on a practical head,[4] he is often within reach of the lowest form of Christians, and in one sentence he will make a truth more clear than others—and those great writers too—can do in some pages.

4. His style is savoury to a spiritual taste, and also moving. As he was pious and devote [devout], without affectation, he had a particular talent of handling divine things so as to fix the attention and affect the heart. This *gustus pietatis*[5] that is so discernible in his writings, and for which he was so famous, is a clear evidence of a rich stock of grace and a large unction from the Holy One.

5. His style is grave and sober, not light and vain. He does not affect that false kind of eloquence that is the idol of some, which is full of swelling words, bold figures. harsh and

---

[4] Section of the discourse.
[5] Latin: taste of piety.

Epistle to the Reader

dangerous phrases sometimes bordering on blasphemy. Such writings are unsavoury to serious people and make the authors contemptible among the wise and judicious. Our author is more intent upon the matter than the style, and he speaks the words of truth and soberness—serious words, that suit the weightiest of all subjects that ever the tongues and pens of men were employed about.

❈ ❈ ❈

As to these sermons,[6] this may commend them, that the Lord Jesus is exalted in them in a lively, spiritual way. That which is the scope of the whole gospel is their great design, *viz.*, to commend a Saviour to the lost world, to magnify his name, and diffuse the savour of his good ointment among the children of men. I shall take notice of a few things in them, more particularly:

1. The oneness of Christ's person is here asserted, against some ancient heretics, justly condemned by the Church many ages ago.

2. He presses prayer much, an exercise of unspeakable advantage and attended with rich and glorious incomes when rightly gone about.

3. The nature of faith is also opened up in a very instructive way, with the various respects under which it acts upon a Mediator. And several questions relating to it are judiciously solved in a way consonant to the holy Scriptures, the analogy of faith and the experience of saints in all ages. Our author is not for new lights—neither the new lights of sectaries nor the new lights of heretics, nor new notions of faith. He tells with a becoming assurance and satisfaction that the faith he commends is as old as Abel.

---

[6] The discourses making up *The Power of Faith and Prayer.*

4. He makes faith to be the condition of the covenant of grace, but in a sound and safe sense, as our greatest and best divines have done. Faith may be called the condition of the covenant betwixt Christ and his people as it is the mean and instrument of the application of his righteousness to elect sinners—the saving mean that unites them to Christ, and instates and interests them in him and his righteousness.

5. Our author has something against separation. He tells us it wants [lacks] all warrant of precept, promise and practice in the Old and New Testament.[7]

⁂

Let us excite ourselves unto godliness. It has many promises—the promises of the life that now is and of that which is to come. It is great gain and has great reward. The power of religion is the main thing: whatever debates be among us, let not this be neglected. Let men pretend [claim] as highly as they will to strictness and zeal for God and his interest, without this they are nothing: God regards not the speech of men but the power, and his kingdom consists not in word but in power (1 Corinthians 4:19–20). God's favour is the best security, living by faith is the greatest wisdom, and to please God is true strictness.

Happy are they who hold fast Christ's name and keep the word of his patience under all changes, whatever may befall them. Light shall arise to them in darkness. They shall have contentment, joy, and comfort—things that vastly surpass all temporal privileges. The peace of God 'that passeth all understanding' shall keep their 'hearts and minds through Christ

---

[7] N.B.: Rutherford is speaking of schismatic separation. For a fuller discussion of the matter, the reader is referred to 'The Doctrine of the visible church' by James Walker in *The Theology and Theologians of Scotland 1560–1750*, chapter IV (Edinburgh: Knox Press, 1982).

Epistle to the Reader

Jesus' (Philippians 4:7). The love of Christ, which passes knowledge, shall be shed abroad in their hearts (Romans 5:5). It is our interest to keep clean garments and walk uprightly. There is neither comfort nor credit to be had by turning aside unto crooked ways. If we lose anything for Christ, he can make it up an hundredfold, even in this life, as he has promised (Mark 10:30; Luke 18:29–30), and give life eternal in the world to come. Christ has the seven spirits of God, and such as adhere to him may expect a double portion of his grace and consolation. Darkness may cover the earth, and gross darkness the people, but the glory of the Lord shall rise upon them.

It is honourable to abide with Christ in his temptations and it is richly rewarded—Christ appoints unto such a kingdom, and they shall be honoured to eat and drink with him at his table (Luke 22:29–30). And it may be he will keep them from the hour of temptation when it is sent upon the world to try others. He may hide them in the day of his anger and feed them with hidden manna, and give them the white stone and the new name. He may guide them by his counsel, till at last he makes them pillars in the temple of God, where they shall go out no more. Reader, that you may enter into that temple and abide therein for ever is the earnest prayer of a well-wisher to you and to the Israel of God.

Rev. Allan Logan

Introduction

AND WHEN JESUS departed thence, two blind men followed him, crying, and saying, 'Thou Son of David, have mercy on us. And when he was come into the house, the blind men came to him: and Jesus saith unto them, 'Believe ye that I am able to do this?' They said unto him, 'Yea, Lord.' Then touched he their eyes saying, 'According to your faith be it unto you.' And their eyes were opened; and Jesus straitly charged them, saying, 'See that no man know it.' But they, when they were departed, spread abroad his fame in all that country. (Matthew 9:27–31).

None of the other evangelists relates this miracle. It was wrought when Christ was returned from the country of the Gergesenes, where he had healed two men possessed with devils, when he returned to Capernaum.

These are the parts of the story:
1. The occasion, or time, when he departed thence.
2. The subjects of the miracle—two blind men.
3. Their behaviour—
    They follow and pray.
    Their vehemence in prayer (they cry).
    The matter of their prayer.
    They persist in their request and pray instantly as they follow him to the house.
4. The qualification Christ requires of them—faith in his omnipotence: 'Believe ye that I am able to do this?'

The Power of Faith and Prayer

5. The blind men's confession of their faith: 'Yea, Lord.'
6. The cure itself—
   The action.
   The words.
   The effect.
7. Christ enjoins secrecy on them: 'See that no man know it.'[8]
8. Their disobedience: 'They ... spread abroad his fame.'

---

[8] The headings of parts 7 and 8 are included here for completeness. As mentioned in the Preface, the work was published in an incomplete form.

Chapter 1

The occasion, or time, when Christ departed

WHEN HE IS in Capernaum, he goes into Matthew's house, not for bodily refreshment but to gain publicans and sinners. Christ the Physician loves to sit upon the sick sinner's bedside, to be nearby to feel his pulse. When he was there, the disciples of John and the Pharisees, offended with Christ's feasting, move the question touching his not fasting. Ere the conference ends, Jairus comes to him for his daughter. In the very way to the maid, he cures the woman diseased twelve years of a bloody issue. In the meantime, Jairus' daughter dies, and Christ raises her. Now coming from this and returning to the house, the two blind men meet him, and that same day he casts out a dumb devil, and so spends the day doing good.

We are to follow and imitate Christ. Christ did good and saved the world, and went about doing good—not so much as a free agent, as by a holy necessity of nature, just as the sun has not liberty to move and to cast its influence of heat and life on the earth but does this by nature. The clouds, when the Lord milks them, must let down rain to nourish the things that grow— Nature forces this, and fat and oily meadows cannot but send forth sweet flowers, delicious herbs and grass. Nature is a strong agent, and cannot be resisted. So, though Christ did good freely and deliberately, yet goodness and grace were in Christ—as with Nature, he could not choose but do good. Grace was in him as a river, he could not keep it within the banks, it must flow over to needy sinners. It's as kindly [natural] to grace in Christ to vent itself for the good of sinners as for the floods to move and run and the fire to cast heat. Come near Christ, cold and dead sinners, and he must warm you. Three sorts of occasions prove that Christ's water of life must continually flow.

(1) In all places he preached and wrought miracles, upon sea and land.

(2) In mountain and valley, in house and field—
    (i) In private with his disciples, in public in the temple.
    (ii) Upon all civil or religious opportunities—at the marriage feast he turned water into wine, at a dinner with Simon the Pharisee he spreads his bowels out to the woman that did wash his feet with tears. He kept all the feasts at Jerusalem. There was a great fishing for souls, and there Christ casts out his lines.
    (iii) At all times, night and day, even sleeping in the ship, he is working a miracle. Christ was greedy of glory to him that sent him: He died praying for sinners.

Let us learn hence that our time is short and eternity is long.

(1) Let us learn to lay up in store, as in a treasure, a good foundation (of many good works) against the time to come, that we may lay hold on eternal life (1 Timothy 6:19). Solomon says (Ecclesiastes 11:2) to these who think that, if we give to many in necessity, we may soon turn poor ourselves, 'Give a portion to seven, and also to eight.' 'Blessed are ye that sow beside all waters' (Isaiah 32:20)—it is spoken of Christ's ministry in the gospel, when multitudes shall be converted, but it holds forth

Chapter 1. The occasion, or time, when Christ departed

that it is a blessing to use opportunity and to enrich ourselves with good works.

(2) If we would have a large stock of many good works to go to heaven with us, let us get grace and the love of Christ. Grace brings forth (as a broody mother) children every day, every hour. Grace works ardently, as does nature. Hence the saints this way do good, the gracious spirit in his own element, when he is in God, meditating in the law of the Lord day and night (Psalm 1:2)—his leaf shall not wither (verse 3). 'At midnight I will rise to give thanks unto thee because of thy righteous judgments. I prevented the dawning of the morning, and cried: I hoped in thy word' (Psalm 119:62, 147). So long as the blood is hot, grace is in action: 'I will sing unto the Lord as long as I live: I will sing praise to my God while I have my being' (Psalm 104:33). Psalm 146:2 has the same: 'While I live I will praise the Lord: I will sing praises unto my God while I have any being.' Anna, a widow of eighty-four years of age, departed not from the temple (Luke 2:37) 'but served God with fastings and prayers night and day'. Paul at Ephesus speaks thus to the elders (Acts 20:31), 'Therefore watch, and remember, that by the space of three years I ceased not to warn every one night and day with tears.'

(3) Evangelical commands run thus (1 Corinthians 15:58): 'Therefore, my beloved brethren, be ye stedfast, unmoveable, always abounding'—in Greek, like a flowing river or fountain—'in the work of the Lord.' 'Rejoice evermore. Pray without ceasing. In every thing give thanks' (1 Thessalonians 5:16–18). And how ardently would Paul have Timothy 'preach the word; be instant' or (in Greek) stand over them—'in season, out of season' (2 Timothy 4:2). And he craves of the rich in this world 'that they be rich in good works' (1 Timothy 6:18). Ah! many (I fear) have a thin and lean stock of good works to

take to heaven with them: Familists[9] teach, that to take delight in the holy service of God is to go a whoring from God!

---

[9] Members of the sect called The Family of God. This mystical, antinomian sect originated in Holland and gained many adherents in England in the sixteenth and seventeenth centuries. They held that religion consisted chiefly in the exercise of love and that absolute obedience was due to all established governments, however tyrannical. Rutherford wrote against their tenets in *A survey of the spiritual antichrist, opening the secrets of familisme and antinomianisme* (London, 1648).

Chapter 2

The subject of the miracle—two blind men

TWO BLIND MEN followed him. Bodily blindness is a sad condition, for they are not masters of their own feet to walk out the way, and they are deprived of many creature comforts that we enjoy and so they are no better than if they were in a dungeon or dark prison.

All that came to Christ and were cured in their souls were for the most part pressed with bodily diseases. Most, of all that came, obtained mercy to their souls; their faith saved them. Some, who were not pressed with the sense of affliction, but came in their prosperity (for aught we know) got no grace to their souls, as the young man who was very rich and the young man who sought leave to go first and bury his father—we do not read of their following Christ. Lest we may think prosperity and riches do close up the way to Christ, the Lord converted Matthew and Zaccheus also.

Now this sad affliction chases the blind men to Christ. They hear that he is a Saviour that cures many the like of them. The way between nature and Christ is the cross, and the way between Christ and glory is also the cross. Sanctified afflictions lead men to God. The forlorn son, pinched with hunger, makes home [returns] to his father's house.

(a) There is something of nature in this. Distressed nature has some weak, dark, midnight thoughts of God. Nature, weeping, has some thoughts that God can help.

(b) He helps others, why not me also?

(c) It sees mercy reaching a hand to misery in the pit. 'From heaven did the Lord behold the earth'—and the first look is mercy—'to hear the groaning of the prisoner; to loose those that are appointed to death' (Psalm 102:19–20). 'The Lord openeth the eyes of the blind' (Psalm 146:8). 'In thee the fatherless findeth mercy' (Hosea 14:3).

Afflictions have some law-plea against the guilty conscience, and advocate against sin. Joseph's brethren are in distress; affliction makes a home-report to them. 'And they said one to another, We are verily guilty concerning our brother, in that we saw the anguish of his soul, when he besought us, and we would not hear; therefore is this distress come upon us' (Genesis 42:21). When Manasseh is among the thorns, his fetters speak to him of his bloodshed. When you see the portrait of a friend well known to you, the friend comes into your mind, because the one is like the other. Affliction and sin are near of kin and like each other. The visage of the cross, black and sour, brings to the memory the ill of sin. Death is the portraiture of sin; the ill of sin and the ill of punishment are both of one colour, and have sour visages.

Sanctified straits cause the conies to run into their rocks for refuge, as many lost strayers from God learn the gate [way] to Christ by their sufferings.

But our sinful abusing of affliction is here rebuked:

(a) We are more sensible of bodily straits than soul plagues. The Pharisees had a more dangerous soul blindness than this bodily blindness, yet it does not chase them to Christ. We are more flesh and bones than spirit and life of Christ.

(b) Afflictions, as afflictions, do not work our return to Christ; because then all afflictions would convert us, but

Chapter 2. The subject of the miracle—two blind men

many are stricken and yet do not return. Then the heaviest affliction would most compel us, but the plague of a hard heart—the heaviest cross—we see, does it not, and yet blind eyes do it. Things nearer to our senses, and things seen, work more on us than the things that are not seen. We labour more for fear of bodily want—for the meat that perisheth—than for the food that endureth to everlasting life (John 6:27). So Christ pleads with the Jews (John 5:44), 'How can ye believe, which receive honour one of another, and seek not the honour that cometh from God only?'. The reason is, we trade more by senses and the flesh. A gracious spirit trades not by sense. Faith is factor [business agent] for the saints; it is their bill of exchange for sums and commodities from heaven. Moses feared not the wrath of the king (Hebrews 11:27) because faith traffics [acts] for him— he endured as seeing him that is invisible.

We have in the mind false opinions of afflictions, as I have elsewhere cleared [made clear], and so they work not rightly [aright] on us.

Chapter 3

The behaviour of the blind men

THERE ARE FOUR PARTS to their behaviour:

1. They follow and pray.
2. Their vehemence in prayer—they cry.
3. The matter of their prayer—'thou Son of David'.
4. They persist in their request and pray instantly—they follow him to the house.

Part 1: They follow and pray

They followed him, crying. Now follows the behaviour of the blind men. The following of faith presses out, praying to the Son of David, of which we are to consider that praying is the birth of faith. 'I believed, therefore have I spoken' (Psalm 116:10). A dumb-born faith is not a true faith. 'But I trusted in thee, O Lord' (Psalm 31:14)—and what did that bring forth? It brought forth prayer. Faith is often with child of [pregnant with] prayer, and prayer with child of faith. 'I said, Thou art my God. Deliver me from the hand of mine enemies. Make thy face to shine upon me' (Psalm 31:14–16), and 'Our fathers trusted in thee: they trusted, and thou didst deliver them' (Psalm 22:4). And upon trusting follows praying—'they cried

Chapter 3. *The behaviour of the blind men*

unto thee, and were delivered' (Psalm 22:5). And again there is a circular generation [begetting] here, for prayer produces faith. The father of the child possessed with a dumb devil 'cried out, and said with tears, Lord, I believe; help thou mine unbelief' (Mark 9:24).

The disciples pray, 'Lord increase our faith.' It is here, as when water pursueth [produces] ice, and again ice produceth water; and vapours gender [engender] clouds and rain, and clouds and rain gender vapours. And it is so in the blind men. They believe in the Son of David, therefore they cry and pray, 'Have mercy on us, Son of David,' and their praying brings forth believing, that Christ is able to heal their blind eyes. It teaches us not to separate praying and believing: praying without faith is breathing of wind, and sounds without life. It is like the wind of bellows, which is not hot of itself, yet it makes heat and foments fire. But praying with faith is like the breathings of a living man, that is hot and nourishes life, and keeps the body in a vital heat of life as long as it continues in the body.

Oh! how many heathenish, pagan sounds in prayer do we utter to our Lord? Prayer without faith is but pagan-service and the voice of dogs howling for hunger. And faith that cannot vent itself in prayer is presumption possessed with a dumb devil.

The country [national] language of faith and the proper grammar of it is prayer. The blind men cry not one only, or one for his fellow, or in the name of both—but both pray. One cries, 'Son of David,' and the other cries, 'Son of David.' Solomon says, 'Two are better than one,' and it is so here. 'Again I say unto you,' says Christ, 'that if two of you shall agree on earth as touching any thing that they shall ask, it shall be done for them of my Father which is in heaven' (Matthew 18:19). Two disciples going to Emmaus confer together of the sufferings of Christ, and Christ comes in as third man. How much more will the Lord hear ten, fifty, an hundred, a whole nation? Every one should stir up another. Many going through a water together are stronger against the stream, and the stronger keep the weaker from drowning. Many coals united make the stronger fire.

The devil is like the barking dog that scatters the sheep. Separation from the assembly of the saints is not of God, especially to refuse to join in prayer with such as they know to be saints—it wants all warrant of precept, promise or practice in the Old or New Testament.

How sweet is that: 'Ten men shall take hold of the skirt of him that is a Jew, saying, We will go with you: for we have heard that God is with you' (Zechariah 8:23). That is, men shall join themselves to the true Church of God. And, 'Then they that feared the Lord spake often one to another: and the Lord hearkened, and heard it' (Malachi 3:16). Yea, we are to believe that Christ is not a Mediator for one, but that he is a National Mediator: so shall Christ sprinkle many nations with his blood (Isaiah 52:15). 'In that day there shall be a root of Jesse, which shall stand for an ensign of the people; to it shall the Gentiles seek: and his rest shall be glorious' (Isaiah 11:10).

Part 2: Their vehemence in prayer

Two blind men follow him, crying. The ardency and heat of the blind men's affection is expressed by crying. Hence these four considerations of crying to God.

1. There may be much crying with the voice where there is not much praying. David's enemies in trouble cried, but there was none to save them (Psalm 18:41), 'even unto the Lord, but he answered them not'. For the young ravens cry to God (Psalm 147:9) yet they pray not. Micah (3:4) speaking of the oppressors says, 'Then shall they cry unto the Lord, but he will not hear them: he will even hide his face from them at that time, as they have behaved themselves ill in their doings.' 'Though

Chapter 3. The behaviour of the blind men

they shall cry unto me, I will not hearken' (Jeremiah 11:11). 'When they fast, I will not hear their cry' (Jeremiah 14:12).

2. There may be no crying with the voice where there is vehement praying, as Hannah prayed and poured out her soul before the Lord (1 Samuel 1:15). This was heart-crying. 'Now Hannah, she spake in her heart; only her lips moved, but her voice was not heard' (verse 13).

There may be much praying where there is no crying. In some prayers, there is much tongue, little spirit and life; so, in some others there is much spirit, little tongue. Light sorrow will speak; extreme grief is dumb and cannot command one word, The deepest floods in their motion speak least, and slide down their banks without noise; shallow brooks flow with great tumbling and din. Some desires are above words, and come out in nothing but in sad sighs and deep groans (Romans 8:26–27). And the Spirit of Christ is as often wrapped in a sigh and in a breathing (Lamentations 3:56), in a panting (Psalms 42:1, 119:131), and in gaping,[10] as in set and instructed prayers. When the troubled soul is speaking to God (Psalm 77:3–4), he says he cannot speak: 'My spirit was overwhelmed. Thou holdest mine eyes waking: I am so troubled that I cannot speak.'

The remnants of a saved and humble Church, they mourn for their iniquities, every one like doves in the valley (Ezekiel 7:16)—that is a weak, low voice. The oppressed Church confessing their sins says, as much as when the voice is low and weak as a dove's voice, there may be great and loud heart shouts. 'We roar all like bears, and mourn sore like doves: we look for judgment, but there is none. For our transgressions are multiplied' (Isaiah 59:11–12).

3. An aim to look or cry to God is welcome. Yea, a look in faith will as soon come to heaven and before the Throne, as a

---

[10] Opening the mouth.

The Power of Faith and Prayer

hideous shout. Jonah in the belly of death could not conveniently cry, yet he said, 'Out of the belly of hell cried I, and thou heardest my voice' (Jonah 2:2), and 'Yet I will look again toward thy holy temple' (verse 4). As hardly [with great difficulty] could he open his eyelids within the belly of the whale, nor could he know well east from west to pray toward the temple; but if he vocally prayed, it was a miracle and therefore his look must be but an aim to lift his eyes to God. 'Therefore I will look unto the Lord' (Micah 7:7); see also Isaiah 8:17.

4. The right crying is that which has an experimental back look to God. 'In my distress I called upon the Lord, and cried unto my God: he heard my voice out of his temple' (Psalm 18:6). The heart crying has good success in heaven, and leaves an impression on the heart, an heart monument never to be forgotten. 'In the day when I cried thou answeredst me, and strengthenedst me with strength in my soul' (Psalm 138:3). 'O Lord my God, I cried unto thee, and thou hast healed me' (Psalm 30:2).

The more that heart crying in faith is opposed and borne down, the stronger it is. Two blind men sitting by the wayside cry to Christ. 'And the multitude rebuked them, because they should hold their peace: but they cried the more, saying, Have mercy on us, O Lord, thou Son of David' (Matthew 20:31). Sure grace cannot be overwhelmed. Prayer is heaven, and hell cannot subdue heaven.

The fervent crying is resolved upon beforehand. 'Evening and morning, and at noon, will I pray, and cry aloud' (Psalm 55:17). Crying that is occasioned by a new and unlooked-for hazard is to be suspected.

Ardent and assiduous crying is of the right stamp, though not heard. 'I have cried day and night before thee' (Psalm 88:1).

When depths of affliction do not so overwhelm the spirit, but the child of God has strength of faith to cry, it is good. 'Out

Chapter 3. The behaviour of the blind men

of the depths have I cried unto thee, O Lord' (Psalm 130:1). When David's breath was cold, and he is rubbing skins with the grave, he says, 'Unto thee will I cry, O Lord my rock: be not silent to me: lest, if thou be silent to me, I become like them that go down into the pit' (Psalm 28:1). Affliction so breaks the soul's strength, that some have no strength to cry, and they lose heart and words to pray, 'Son of David, have mercy on us.'

Part 3: The matter of their prayer

The third thing to be considered in the blind men's behaviour to Christ is the matter of their prayer. In which you have:

1. The person they pray to, the Son of David.
2. The petition: 'Have mercy on us.'

1. The person they pray to, the Son of David

In this, consider that Christ must be God, for the blind men set him in the throne of him that hears prayers. They believe his omnipotence, that he can give eyes to the blind, which God only can do (Psalm 146:8). Consider also that he must be man, because he is David's son, and the promise of the blessed Messiah by covenant was made unto David (2 Samuel 7:12).

Consider also that the stability of David's kingdom was in Christ. 'I have made a covenant with my chosen, I have sworn unto David my servant, Thy seed will I establish for ever, and build up thy throne to all generations. Once have I sworn by my holiness that I will not lie unto David. His seed shall endure for ever, and his throne as the sun before me' (Psalm 89:3–4, 35–36). Peter says, 'David, being a prophet, and knowing that God had sworn with an oath to him, that of the fruit of his loins, according to the flesh, he would raise up Christ to sit on his throne' (Acts 2:30–31), and spoke of his resurrection. He 'was made of the seed of David' (Romans 1:3).

Hence, first a word about the person, and then a word about the nature of man—David's Son.

The person of Christ

A word about the person. Every man naturally born of a woman has a natural personship [personality] of his own and subsists by himself, but God, assuming man's nature, took the nature but did not assume man's personship, for then he behoved to lay aside his own personship and assume our personship, But it was not good that Christ should lay aside any thing that he had from eternity. We had need of his person, in the mediation between God and us. There is refuse in us, but nothing to be casten [cast] away in Christ. Both the nature and person of the Son of God was of good use for us—it was the Godhead that only could make his blood to be the blood of God and perfume it with infinite merit, so as God took of his own to satisfy himself, the Godhead augmented the price to an infinite sum.

The Manhood[11] had not strength against infinite wrath. The Godhead by acting, and the active influence of grace, strength, faith, comfort to suffer, was from the Godhead without any receiving of suffering or passion at all in the Godhead.

No strength but God's strength could overcome the devil and sin, hell, and death, for we were under these. And a stronger One, as strong as God, must take captives by strong hand from these enemies. Nothing that sins and can die can overcome the first tempter to sin, any more than one under sin who loses his strength by sin can come out by his own strength from under sin; nor can one that is under death come from under death (Romans 1:4; Hebrews 2:14), for we loss [lose] strength by sinning and dying.

---

[11] The human nature of Christ.

Chapter 3. The behaviour of the blind men

We must have such a Saviour as can possess us with the salvation he has purchased; else, if he could but say to the prisoners, 'Go forth!' and not put them in actual possession of their liberty, he should be but a half Saviour and a lame Redeemer, as Arminians make him. Now, if he be a perfect Saviour, he must be God—firstly to steward and give out grace and the gifts of the Holy Ghost, and secondly to put the captives in possession of eternal glory he must have the keys of both kingdoms, of the kingdom of grace and the kingdom of glory. If Christ had kept both his own personality and also assumed ours, Christ should have been two persons, two Sons, two Saviours. Now, there is but one Son of God, one Mediator, one Saviour, and he has not a marrow [counterpart] nor equal besides. There is but one 'I' (Isaiah 43:11): 'I, even I, am the Lord; and beside me there is no Saviour', and it is our comfort that it is so. Christ God assumed our singular nature in his own personality, and shifted [rejected] our personship and refused it.

Now, man's nature subsists personally with the nature of the Son of God in the subsistence and personship of the Son of God. This is the greatest wonder in heaven, that man is made the same 'I' and person with God—not formally, but in union. There is but one single 'I', one personship between both the Godhead and the Manhood, but that is a strong one. The Manhood lives, loves, knows, breathes, speaks, in the bosom, in the sea, in the great ocean of the infinite personality of God, and is not swallowed up of it but remains in that heaven with all the entire nature and natural properties of man—perfect man as we are, sin excepted. As if, out of the root and body of the fairest cedar, the Lord should cause a thorn tree to grow and blossom, having life and subsistence in the root and body of the cedar. Or as if there were a sweet delicious rose that should spread its fair, ruddy leaves to the four corners of the world and cast a shadow over the little globe of the earth; and upon the stalk and out of the root of this rose should grow a little, poor, tender lily, having no life, no growing or subsistence, but in the stalk and root of this rose. So here the Son of God, the Rose of Glory, green, fair and ruddy from generation to generation, more than the glory of Sharon, in the fullness of time, without change or shadow of change, assumed our nature, and a tender twig, a flower, a lily of the house of Jesse grew out of his root, being both the root and the offspring of David—the Manhood grows and lives in the same stalk with the nature of God.

Angels think it their new heaven (1 Peter 1:12), above their old heaven, to draw aside the curtain and look into this wonder of glory. And what joy and happiness must it be in the life to come, to see such an admirable, dainty, excellent wonder, and to touch the boards of this ark. And to what glory can the Lord exalt sinful nature! It is true no created nature can come to so near a communion with God—no, not the highest of angels. But it should warm the thoughts to remember that, when our hidden life shall appear, we shall live, joy, and reign as kings within the bosom of God, within the walls and circuit (to speak so) of joy, when we shall enter as strangers and go in to a king's palace, into the joy of our Lord. And, as the birth is warmed with the heat of the mother, so is the soul taken up and warmed with the love, light and happiness of an immediate vision going about it. If we be now in Christ by faith—and it is our happiness to be—then we shall be in Christ in a vision of glory, in a far higher manner and measure.

The essence and nature of God did not simply, as nature, assume the Manhood, for then should the Father and Holy Ghost (which have the very same nature, and no other nature, with the Son) have been incarnate; but the nature as personalised in the Son only, did assume our nature. All the three were actors in the incarnation, but then the 'I' Son only did assume and take on our nature.

Chapter 3. The behaviour of the blind men

The human nature of Christ

A word about the nature of man—David's Son. 'David's Son' speaks [bespeaks] the lowly and lovely condescension of God. David was a sinful man, guilty of adultery and of treacherous murdering of Uriah, and conceived in sin. And Rahab was a harlot and a Gentile. But the Son of God would marry his holy and spotless nature with the nature of sinners in a personal union.

You see, man could ascend no higher than to come so near to God, and that God could descend no lower than to assume a tent of clay from the loins of sinful men. Christ is the fittest mids [mediator] by participation of both extremes to friend [befriend] God and man. He is the common march-stone [boundary stone] and the place of assembly, and it is fit that his person should be the place of treaty for both parties.

But there were reasons grave and weighty why Christ should be a man. He must be a king to fill King David's Chair of State—a stranger could not reign over us. 'I have exalted one chosen out of the people' (Psalm 89:19). 'Their nobles shall be of themselves, and their governor shall proceed from the midst of them' (Jeremiah 30:21). Just as amongst us in Scotland, one that had no title or right to the crown, and not of the royal line, nor of the king's blood, could not be our king—so it was not fit that the king of the redeemed ones should be a usurper.

Christ had both God's right and man's right to the crown. There was none living to whom the crown of Judah was birthright. But this David's Son, he was born with king's blood in his veins. Amongst men, the crown often runs in a wrong blood for the sins of the land, but the womb gives the crown to Christ. 'Thus saith the Lord God; Remove the diadem, and take off the crown: this shall not be the same: exalt him that is low, and abase him that is high. I will overturn, overturn,

The Power of Faith and Prayer

overturn, it: and it shall be no more until he come whose right it is; and I will give it him' (Ezekiel 21:26–27).

It is a plague to a land that the crown should come through the hands of strangers and uncouth men. When the Messiah comes, the crown is upon the right head. It is a singular comfort that Christ has law to reign over me; I am his own, he will not crush his own. Christ has no law or right to be king of devils and unbelievers. Woe be to these that are strangers to Christ! Christ has no law to be a crown and sceptre over you, but he is born to be a rod of iron to break you in pieces.

Christ behoved to be a prophet that had the language to speak in a known tongue to the elect. 'I will raise them up a Prophet from among their brethren, like unto thee, and will put my words in his mouth' (Deuteronomy 18:18). Did not God put his words in the mouths of Moses, Samuel, David and Isaiah, yea even in the mouth of Amos a herdsman? Yea, but words fit to turn the heart, a language to the soul that the sheep of Christ, and they only, could know and follow, was only in Christ's mouth. It is all gibberish and barbarian language that prophets or apostles speak to the heart, until Christ gives out the word—the heart of the Beloved knows the voice of her husband among a thousand, 'the voice of my beloved' (Song 2:8).

God ordered it so, that the high priest was a born Israelite, by birth a son of Aaron. Christ must be one of our house. If our High Priest had been an angel, he could not have sighed and prayed for us with a man's heart, he could not have lifted up man's hands to heaven, he could not have wept and shed tears with man's eyes for us, he could not then have been a merciful High Priest. He might have been the Lord, merciful and gracious, but our High Priest must have (Hebrews 2:17) a man's bowels, a man's affections of sorrow, sadness, pity, love, fear, desire, joy, to offer a sacrifice and prayers for us. And the sacrifice and prayers must be offered with man's mercy, and

Chapter 3. The behaviour of the blind men

man's feeling, and man's yearning of bowels. 'For we have not an high priest which cannot be touched with the feeling of our infirmities; but was in all points tempted like as we are, yet without sin' (Hebrews 4:15). Then if there were not a man's heart in heaven, and man's bowels, and a feeling and tempted Saviour in heaven, he could not be a fit High Priest.

Christ had my nature with its sinless affections. There is one of our kin and house in heaven, of the same blood. And the apostle infers that then we may be homely and familiar with God. 'Let us therefore come boldly unto the throne of grace, that we may obtain mercy, and find grace to help in time of need' (Hebrews 4:16). I deserve no mercy, and therefore the sinner has a sort of unbelieving shamefacedness, a sinful shyness, a trepidation and fearfulness to go near God, or to come with boldness within sight of the throne. Why? Because I am sinful and unworthy.

There are two things in our text that should remove our estranging fears.

1. In the first place, nature teaches men not to be feared [afraid] at the brother though he be a king. Why! he lay in the same womb with you. Then go boldly and confidently to him. Oneness of blood makes boldness naturally. Yea, you may be more homely with Christ than with your born brother:

(a) Because if your brother were a king and you but a low, poor man, pride might overcome nature and make him not take it well that you use him as a brother, for he is now your king—and honour can change manners and nature in sinful men. Now, natural affection in Christ, because he is a perfect man (and grace sharpens sinless natural affections, sin blunts them), Christ in natural duties cannot come short— Lordship can neither change manners nor nature in him, nor turn off his heart from his poor friends. The love of Christ cannot turn lordly or proud (John 20:17; Matthew 28:10; Acts 9:4; Revelation 1:17, 19:7).

(b) Christ takes it as a favour if you will, with the boldness of faith, claim brotherhood and friendship of him. When the apostle says (Hebrews 2:11), 'For both he that sanctifieth and they who are sanctified are all of one: for which cause he is not ashamed to call them brethren,' he speaks by a figure [figure of speech] (a litotes) that he is not ashamed of his sanctified ones. That is, he thinks it an honour to call them brethren: a king cannot have these thoughts of his brother if he is poor and base.

2. Again, there is another thing in this text. Because I am vile and sinful, I cannot go—far less can I go boldly—to the throne of grace. But we may go boldly. Why? The text says he is a man and a High Priest like unto us, and therefore we have, by law of brotherhood and fraternity, blood-right to mercy and grace, because it is not only the mercy and the grace of a brother, but of a brother who is by law High Priest. Now, the grace of the High Priest, as High Priest, is made over to these for whom he is High Priest. It is a public and relative mercy and grace that is in Christ, not personal and for himself only. Grace is our birthright. Now, this birthright we may not sell. Believers, born in the Church, within the covenant, are of kin to Christ.

The Lord's justice required that the nature that in Adam contracted the debt, and the nature that turned bankrupt, should be the surety and pay the debt. The first Adam made a hole in the world and let in sin; a new king, even sin, did enter in and reign (Romans 5:17). The second Adam—a man like the first in all things, except sin—made up the gap, and God brings in another king that reigns to this day, 'that as sin reigned unto death, even so might grace reign through righteousness unto eternal life by Jesus Christ our Lord' (Romans 5:21). The law was, that the nearest brother and kinsman that was able should redeem his brother's mortgaged lands, for it was most kindly

Chapter 3. The behaviour of the blind men

that the nearest in blood should brook[12] his friend's inheritance because he was born heir to the land.

Adam and his, if they had never sinned, were born heirs of Paradise. Sin sold the land and put out old possessors. There is an heir born of man's house, nearest of blood to us—the Man Christ, God and man, according to both natures, as the Son of God and the Son of man. The highest Paradise was Emmanuel's kindly land: our Kinsman redeemed it back again with a great ransom for our behalf. He 'gave himself a ransom for all, to be testified in due time' (1 Timothy 2:6)—the Brother has made up the house again.

Practical applications

1. You have heaven, O believers, by blood-right. Our Friend is the public and general heir. Glory be to him, who gave a sum of money that was the country-coin [national currency]. He gave his flesh, his body a sweet smelling savour to God (Ephesians 5:2). 'Come in, friends,' says Christ. 'You are no more strangers, but household men, and kindly citizens in heaven; the land is not out of the name.' The Son of man is the new Lord of the new Paradise, who has handselled [purchased] heaven with our flesh, and heaven in him is our freehold. Christ is the sinner's Magna Carta,[13] his new patent, and his flesh is the new Broad Seal,[14] his gospel the new charter.

2. 'He that sanctifieth and they who are sanctified are all of one' (Hebrews 2:11). Grace and the new life are ours by the new birth and a new nature derived from the second Adam. Come, be of Christ's house. Ally with him. Grace and the new life come to us by one of our own flesh. Our blood-friend

---

[12] Have, or enjoy, the use or possession of.

[13] The Magna Carta was a great charter of English personal and political liberty obtained from King John in 1215. The term is used figuratively for any important document establishing rights.

[14] The official seal of the nation: the Great Seal.

takes us in to be heirs of an immortal life. Christ asks not what Amorite was your father. So we come in to the new stock, to David's house, and mix with the king's blood, and be born again, not of blood, nor of the will of man (John 1:13).

2. The petition: 'Have mercy on us'

'Have mercy on us.' They say not, 'Lord, open our eyes,' but 'Have mercy on us.' When the women of Canaan prays for her possessed daughter (Matthew 15:22), she bottoms [bases] all on this: 'Have mercy on me, O Lord, thou Son of David.' David is weak and sore afflicted, and his prayer is: 'Have mercy upon me, O Lord: for I am weak.' 'Have mercy upon me, O Lord, for I am in trouble' (Psalm 31:9).

There is good reason for this grammar.

(a) First, whole eyes, seeing eyes alone, are one thing, and the mercy of seeing eyes is another thing. The single creature[15] is one thing, but the creature given in God's mercy is another thing. Oft we seek from God but the scabbard, the outside of the blessing—and that is but half a blessing— but mercy and God's mercy is the lining, the inside, the soul of the blessing.

David (Psalm 21) makes it a blessing to be established in his throne, but not of itself: 'For the king trusteth in the Lord, and through the mercy of the most High he shall not be moved' (verse 7).

The 57th Psalm is penned when David fled from Saul in the cave, and he had need of King Saul's mercy to spare his life. But he looks higher. 'Be merciful unto me, O God, be merciful unto me' (verse 1). David's soul was among lions. In faith he believed deliverance—but how believed he? God

---

[15] The creature on its own.

Chapter 3. The behaviour of the blind men

would send a messenger to deliver. Therefore he says, 'God shall send forth his mercy and his truth' (verse 3).

Elisabeth had been barren and had no child. How does the Lord cure that? In mercy when she brings forth a son, the Holy Ghost thus expresses it (Luke 1:58), 'And her neighbours and her cousins heard how the Lord had shewed great mercy upon her; and they rejoiced with her.'

When Lot is come out of Sodom, he says (Genesis 19:19), 'Behold now, thy servant hath found grace in thy sight, and thou hast magnified thy mercy, which thou hast shewed unto me in saving my life.'

(b) Mercy is infinitely above seeing eyes. We may have mercy, and want seeing eyes and hearing ears, and be happy. Therefore, when God says he will correct David's seed when they sin, and punish them with the rod of men, there is a gracious 'nevertheless' added (Psalm 89:33): 'Nevertheless my lovingkindness will I not utterly take from him, nor suffer my faithfulness to fail.' And there is a gracious 'but' added (2 Samuel 7:14–15): 'If he commit iniquity, I will chasten him with the rod of men, and with the stripes of the children of men: but my mercy shall not depart away from him, as I took it from Saul.' And more cannot be holden [held] forth and given to everyone that thirsts, and is invited to come to the waters, than this (Isaiah 55:3): 'I will make an everlasting covenant with you, even the sure mercies of David.' And a sadder plague cannot be inflicted on an obstinate people than that which the Lord speaks of by his prophet (Jeremiah 16:5): 'For thus saith the Lord, Enter not into the house of mourning, neither go to lament nor bemoan them: for I have taken away my peace from this people, saith the Lord, even lovingkindness and mercies.'

(c) Praying is a grace, and must be fathered and bottomed on grace. There is no plea nor motive why God should hear us but mercy. I know not whether heaven and the crown, or the holding of the crown of heaven upon the charter of free mercy and the tender bowels of God in Christ, be sweetest, but Christ is born (Luke 1:77–78) 'to give knowledge of salvation ... through the tender mercy of our God'. David in distress (Psalm 4:1) prays, 'Have mercy upon me, and hear my prayer.' Mercy is an enemy to merit. David (Psalm 51:1) prays, 'Have mercy upon me, O God'. He seeks forgiveness of sins. Hence, remission, heaven and glory of themselves were not to be desired but on the terms of mercy. Oh, all in heaven are tenants by mercy: anything better than hell to sinners is mercy. And it is a mercy that the Church is not consumed, because 'his compassions fail not' (Lamentations 3:22) that there is a handful and a seed left. It is a mercy bestowed on a people that was no people (Romans 9:25–26). And the Word will warrant us to say that two seeing eyes are mercy, not merit.

3. How careful should we be to know upon what title we enjoy the common favours of God. The very house and outward blessings of the saints are bemercied (Jeremiah 30:18): 'Thus saith the Lord; Behold, I will bring again the captivity of Jacob's tents, and have mercy on his dwelling places; and the city shall be builded upon her own heap'. What!—is a house, or stones and timber, capable of mercy? Yes, the Lord sprinkles and perfumes things with mercy as well as men, and the Lord denies mercy to children of the wicked in relation to their father. Oh! sad is that prophecy on the enemies of the Lord (Hosea 2:4): 'And I will not have mercy upon her children; for they be the children of whoredoms.' And (Isaiah 9:17): 'Therefore'—because leaders and people go wrong—'the Lord shall have no joy in their young men, neither shall he have mercy on their fatherless and widows.' The king of a sinful people is no mercy, but dipped in wrath (Hosea 13:11): 'I gave thee a

Chapter 3. The behaviour of the blind men

king in mine anger.' He grants to sinners meat that they lust for, but not in mercy (Psalm 78:30–31): 'But while their meat was yet in they mouths, the wrath of God came upon them, and slew the fattest of them.'

By the contrary, when Hezekiah is delivered from death and restored to health and life for fifteen years (Isaiah 38:17): 'Behold, for peace I had great bitterness: but thou hast' bemercied (or beloved, or overloved) 'my soul … from the pit of corruption.' We should weigh outward favours in spiritual balances.

Many care not if they have lumps of strong, healthy bodies and good eyes and hearing ears and perfect senses—and consider not whether they have these bodies in mercy, as temples and dwelling houses for the Holy Ghost. And they are satisfied if they have lively children, but never asked the question, whether they have these children in mercy of no? Or, if they have children, as Ephraim had them (Hosea 9:13): 'But Ephraim shall bring forth his children to the murderer.'

And men are contented if they have wedges of gold, heaps and bags of silver, and affluence of goods, full barns, power, victories and Parliaments. But, ah! they consider not their holding of these, whether these be merciless mercies and graceless favours, or bemercied with the special kindness and favour of God. If you haw mercy to your souls, children, houses, honours, lands, or mercies coming from the bowels of Christ, the good of them cannot be taken away. When the child is taken away from you, you keep the mercy of the child. The lands, the houses, the riches are gone, but the mercy of lands, of the houses or the riches, all the devils in hell cannot take them from you. When children, goods, cattle, flocks, health were taken from Job, the charter on which he had all these remained with him (Job 19:27), for the Redeemer of Job, the great mother mercy, lived. When David lost his kingdom and country, mercy stayed with him (Psalm 57:1, Psalm 23).

Three questions concerning outward favours from God

Ask three questions concerning seeing eyes, health, riches, children, and all outward favours.

1. Whence you have them?—from God as Creator? So an ox and a horse have two seeing eyes; reprobates have flocks of sons and daughters (Job 21:11): 'They send forth their little ones like a flock.' Or have you all these from God in Christ your Redeemer? Know that if your person be in Christ, then your basket and your dough and your table are more to you than to reprobate men. Blessed bread is more than bread, it is the bread of heaven. If bread, health, seeing eyes, children, peace came to you through Christ, David's Son, then they smell of Christ's ointments and perfumes. What Christ gives is more than the single creature. All things are yours. Why? Because you are Christ's (1 Corinthians 3:21). The gift smells of the giver. The muist [musk] of heaven is on all that comes through the sweet-smelling fingers of Christ.

2. See in what title you have them—as mercies or no. And you shall know it, thus is your person bemercied, as Paul says (1 Timothy 1:16), 'I was mercied,' or, 'I obtained mercy.' God can hardly give favours in wrath to a child that is himself a vessel of mercy. The wicked are greedy of the carcase and body of dumb and deaf mercies. They cry, 'Children, Lord, children else I die.' But nothing of mercy to themselves. They say, 'O that God would give me gold and sums of silver,' but never, 'O that the Lord would give me God.' And, 'O for corn, wine and oil,' but never, 'O that the Lord would give me his Son, then he would give me all other things.' A greater favour cannot be thought of than this (1 Peter 2:10): 'Which had not obtained mercy, but now have obtained mercy.' And a sorer plague cannot be than is spoken of (Isaiah 27:11): 'It is a people of no understanding: therefore he that made them will not have mercy on them, and he that formed them will shew them no favour.'

Chapter 3. The behaviour of the blind men

3. Know well to what end you use the outward mercies. If you use youth and health as the ant does the summer—if you provide friends for eternity and employ the tongue to praise and glorify God, not to blaspheme him—then health and tongue look like mercies. Outward favours wasted on our lusts look wrath-like. When a State uses its power and victories to honour God, build his house, defend the godly and the oppressed, then power and victory are given in mercy. When they use their power to rapine, extortion, crushing of the poor, causing the eyes of the needy and of the widow to fail in looking for justice but they have none, then the Lord gives to the land a parliament in his wrath as well as a king.

Part 4: They follow him to the house

'And when he was come into the house, the blind men came to him' (verse 28). Now follows the fourth part of the blind men's behaviour to Christ—they follow him to the house, crying to him.

The blind men pray, and they pursue their prayer with eagerness and constancy. In earnest praying, there are these spiritual ingredients:

1. Vehemence of heart.
2. Fervent prayer or praying from the Spirit.
3. Instancy in prayer.

1. Vehemence of heart

The first ingredient is vehemence of heart—so they cry. If in any work all the heart is required, then it is here. Praying is of kin to the highest, most spiritual and immediate worship that the courtiers of heaven—angels and glorified spirits—perform to God. Now, in praising, they put forth their whole strength, and David on this ground preaches this to the angels (Psalm 103:20): 'Bless the Lord, ye his angels, that excel in strength.' He would say, 'I have neither strength to pray nor praise. O, angels, put forth all your angel power to praise him.' Morally, the creatures can put forth no more strength in praising and praying than they have, and angels put forth all the strength they have in praising. But angels and men, though they should put forth more strength than physically (and either by creation or grace) they have, they would not pay their debt, and never equal God's excellences in praises. But the glorified put forth their strength to the utmost—they both sing and cry (Isaiah 6:3). Yea 'and they rest not day and night, saying, Holy, holy, holy, Lord God Almighty, which was, and is, and is to come' (Revelation 4:8). And one of the angels cried 'with a loud voice to him that sat on the cloud' (Revelation 14:15), praying that the Lord's harvest of wrath may be hastened on the kingdom of Antichrist.

And what are angels, but lumps of burning fire taken up with a desire to have the Lord honoured? And because praying is an adoring of the Most High, then a voice of iron, an hundred tongues in one head, sides of brass were all too little in this service to cry prayers to heaven. Hence, praying in the Word is expressed by knocking, where the strength of the arm is required; instant praying is resembled by the two most masterful elements—fire and water. It is resembled by fire that cannot be kept under (Psalm 39:3): 'My heart was hot within me, while I was musing the fire burned: then spake I with my tongue.' The fire flamed out in praying (verse 4): 'Lord, make me to know mine end, and the measure of my days, what it is.' It is resembled by water, hence that frequent expression, 'to pour out the soul before the Lord'. If the mouth of a vessel full of water be turned up and opened, the water cannot but come out, just as the floods cannot but flow.

Instant praying is called wrestling, as Jacob by prayer wrestled with God. Now, in wrestling, the whole man is employed and all his strength, all the bones, nerves, legs and arms of the soul are set to work in praying.

2. Fervent prayer

There is fervent prayer, or praying from the spirit (James 5:16)—prayer possessed with the spirit, with the whole strength of the soul. The spirit of man is his strength. As the horses of Egypt are flesh and not spirit—that is, weak and not strong—so the spirits and working power of wine is the strength of the wine. The spirits of roses and spices are all their strength. And if a man's spirit be wounded and broken, the man is gone. Jude (verse 20) exhorts them to edify themselves, 'praying in the Holy Ghost', the Spirit being about them as a house and the Holy Spirit not so much in them as they in the Holy Ghost.

3. Instancy in prayer

Beside their crying in prayer, there is a higher part of their instancy in prayer noted—they cried by the way and they follow Christ to the house praying.

Now, we are commanded to pray, continuing in prayer, for the prevalency of praying and the victory is here (Matthew 26:41). He says not, 'Pray,' but, 'Watch and pray, that ye enter not into temptation.' And as praying is a chief part of the armour of God (Ephesians 6), so the Holy Ghost teaches how this armour should be used (verse 18).

(a) Watchfulness and fervour of praying is set down, praying always (Greek: 'in every season')—no occasion of prayer should be omitted.

(b) With all prayer and supplication.

(c) In the Spirit in Greek it has something of the passive verb, being prayed on by the Spirit', thereby showing that the Spirit of adoption is a victorious Spirit and overmasters the soul.

(d) 'Watching thereunto'—the Spirit of prayer sleeps not much.

(e) It goes on, not wearying, watching thereunto with all perseverance, for all the saints (1 Thessalonians 3:10): 'Night and day praying exceedingly that we might see your face, and perfect that which is lacking in your faith.'

You profess that there is life in the play [plea] and a prevailing hope when you watch unto praying (Psalm 22:2): 'O my God, I cry in the daytime, but thou hearest not; and in the night season, and am not silent.' Now he contradicts the flesh in the next words: 'What!—shall I cry night and day and not be heard? As good as sow wheat in the sea sand and wash the Ethiopian as pray? There's no hope that I can be delivered.' He answers, 'Yea, but there is hope. It is not a vain thing to pray night and day, though 'I cry ..., but thou hearest not. But thou art holy, O thou that inhabitest the praises of Israel. Our fathers trusted in thee' (verses 2–4). And that you may know that faith in God is not an empty work, he says it over again, 'They trusted, and thou didst deliver them. They cried unto thee, and were delivered' (verses 4–5). So does the prophet Habakkuk answer doubtings that may arise from a cross [adverse] providence—that the world was as the sea, full of disorders and confusion, in which the great fish eat the small, and the great ones sacrifice to their own net, and they ascribe all to themselves (Habakkuk 1:14–16). I will for all this believe there is hope in Israel concerning this thing: 'I will stand upon my watch, and set me upon the tower, and will watch to see what he will say unto me, and what I shall answer when I am reproved' (chapter 2:1). And the Lord gave him both an answer of joy (verse 3), 'For the vision is yet for an appointed time, but at the end it shall speak, and not lie,' and he gave a counsel, 'Though it tarry, wait for it: because it will surely come, it will not tarry.'

Praying with continuance in prayer argues strong and heavenly desires without fainting. So David (Psalm 130:5): 'I wait for the Lord'—he rises yet higher—'My soul doth wait.' And

Chapter 3. The behaviour of the blind men

because waiting without warrant is but wind, he shows his warrant: his hope has a pass signed by the Lord: 'And in his word do I hope.' Strong are his prayers out of the depths (verse 1). He expresses the strength of his desires (verse 6): 'My soul waiteth for the Lord more than they that watch for the morning.' Psalm 88:1: 'O Lord God of my salvation, I have cried day and night before thee.' Yet (verse 7), 'Thy wrath lieth hard upon me.' Yet to show that he faints not, he says (verse 13), 'But unto thee have I cried, O Lord; and in the morning shall my prayer prevent thee.'

Practical applications

1. This should condemn distracting thoughts and wandering of spirit in prayer. Not only is not the whole man and whole strength not set on work in these prayers, but not any at all of the spirit is there, but the heart gone a-whoring after thoughts of vanity. Now, can the man pour out that which is not within? The spirit is gone out after other lovers, in so far it is a *non ens*;[16] there is not a spirit of adoption within, and therefore he cannot pour it out.

2. Lazy, cold and dead prayers are condemned. Many pray, and care not whether God hears them or no; they pour out, not their desires before the Lord, but naked single words, and do but take the name of God in vain.

3. Many use prayer as sorcerers do a charm. If the charm miscarry when it is used in all its rites, they never use it again. When the king of Moab saw that Balaam had no enchantment against Israel, he sent him away and would use him no more. So, many, when the prayer is once put up to God, if they be not by and by heard, they cannot watch and continue in praying, but pray and sleep: if the charm work not, they must cast about for another wind, and can wait no longer on the Lord.

---

[16] Latin: nonentity; something which has no existence.

But there is a devil that is not cast out, but by fasting and prayer.

4. Though deliverance comes not when the harvest is past and the summer is ended, yet wait for the Lord all the next winter, and wait on, many summers. For:

(a) The Lord is worthy our on-waiting.[17] Say that one saint should live from the creation to the last coming of Christ, and the Spirit and the Bride should all that time pray, 'Come, Lord Jesus', this should be a waiting on for many hundreds of ages—yet should the glory of his appearance and the weight of free salvation be far beyond that painful on-waiting. If a good harvest richly recompenses a long summer's hope, and a shipful of gold from India overbalances [outweighs] a long sea journey, then our on-waiting in prayer and our hope (though it lives while it be grey-headed, even sixty or seventy years) is no loser: when the Lord, who is far more precious than a ship full of gold, must with the sweetness of his presence more than over-satisfy our pains [troubles], And an on-waiting people shall say (as Isaiah 25:9), 'Lo, this is our God; we have waited for him, and he will save us: this is the Lord; we have waited for him, we will be glad and rejoice in his salvation.'

(b) It were not good that Ephraim were taken out of the oven while he is yet a raw cake unturned (Hosea 7:8). It is ill for many that they come raw out of the furnace, and that they come from under the rod while they are yet like sour summer fruit not satisfied with summer sap, and are plucked off the tree before the time. Grapes green and un-ripe, though trodden on, yield no good wine. Patience has but half a work, not its perfect work, when we are delivered but not humbled.

---

[17] Waiting for deliverance.

Chapter 3. The behaviour of the blind men

(c) It is wisdom to refer our time by will unto God, for he has it under his decree by necessity. The Lord's time must be the most seasonable for opening of the graves of dry bones, and our time out of time were the timing of the world in our hand. We are so impatient of providence that we should do as Antichrist does—change times and seasons to the worse; we should appoint another time for summer and winter than God has appointed, and another season for the rising of the sun and the motion of the moon than the Creator has appointed, and the world should be mistimed, for we love to do God's office rather than our own duty. And if we had the timing of our own afflictions and of our deliverances, and of our own heaven, we should both mistime and misplace all, and turn the world upside down. None of God's works are mistimed. There are millions up triumphing before the throne; not one of them came short of heaven half an hour or a minute after due time; not one came a moment sooner than was fit to infinite wisdom. God makes everything beautiful in his time. When the smoke of afflictions is ready to suffocate us, we are as impatient to live, as if it were to be feared: 'If I come not in my own set time that I carve for myself, some other shall have my crown and my heaven over my head.'

Chapter 4

The qualification Christ requires of them— faith in his omnipotence

VERSE 28: 'And Jesus saith unto them, Believe ye that I am able to do this?' We now come to the fourth particular in the text, to wit, the qualification that Christ requires of the blind men, 'Believe ye that I am able to do this?'—in which we have these points to be discussed:

1. Why Christ requires faith of these men before He gave them sight.
2. What faith it is He requires of them.
3. What influence faith has in the working of miracles.

Part 1: Why Christ requires faith of these men before he gave them sight

Why Christ craves faith of them is clear, because many sought of him the benefit of health, who upon mere necessity did it and yet were afraid to profess him to be the Messiah. Now, Christ will have from his followers not a faith in the corner and a night following of Christ, such as was in Nicodemus, but an open, fair, clear confession. Hence this doctrine.

Chapter 4. The qualification Christ requires of them

There is a necessity that not only we believe, but that we profess our faith and confess Christ before men—so Matthew 10:32: 'Whosoever therefore shall confess me before men, him will I confess also before my father which is in heaven.'

This is needful for the following reasons:

1. The covenant of grace obliges us to it. 'One shall say, I am the Lord's and another shall call himself by the name of Jacob; and another shall subscribe with his hand unto the Lord' (Isaiah 44:5). So at Antioch, believers took on them the name of Christians, and as Paul by his calling to be an apostle is said to bear the name of God unto the Gentiles, so are the saints to bear Christ before the world. When believers of old did join themselves to the Church and were baptised, they professed they would carry Christ on their foreheads through the world.

2. The honour of God and his name obliges us to this. Moses when he was come to age, thinking it a reproach to be called an Egyptian, refused to be called the son of Pharoah's daughter—what then?—but chose rather to suffer affliction with the people of God. It might seem no great business whose son he be, so he be God's son, but he would be [wished to be] called a son of Zion, for so he was. And every man by his place is to profess what he is. The son is not to deny his father, or a citizen his country; nor is a servant to be ashamed of his master, except he be a vile man, and then he should labour to vindicate himself. This was Peter's and the apostles' sin, when their Master was within a step or two of hanging and shame, they stole away from him and left him alone. Christ willed them not to fight for him, but yet to confess him they were obliged.

3. It is an honour that Christ says he graces his servants with. 'Him that overcometh will I make a pillar in the temple of my God' (Revelation 3:12). 'And ye shall leave your name for a curse unto my chosen: for the Lord God shall slay thee, and call his servants by another name' (Isaiah 65:15). So John sees

the Church of God in a vision (Revelation 14:1): 'And I looked, and, lo, a Lamb stood on the mount Sion, and with him an hundred forty and four thousand, having his Father's name written in their foreheads.' So the saints go to heaven with Christ on their foreheads in a visible profession, that all that see them shall call them 'The holy people, The redeemed of the Lord: and thou shalt be called, Sought out, A city not forsaken' (Isaiah 62:12).

4. It is an honourable thing to God; yet the confession of God before men adds no real glory to God, nor any worship or service we can do—only it puts a lustre on his glory before men and angels by way of declaration. Now the Lord promises a real honour for a name honour (to speak so): 'Whosoever therefore shall confess me before men, him will I confess also before my Father which is in heaven' (Matthew 10:32). 'Keep sound wisdom and discretion' (Proverbs 3:21)—and verse 22: 'so shall they be life unto thy soul, and grace to thy neck.' Wisdom (Proverbs 4:9) 'shall give to thine head an ornament of grace: a crown of glory shall she deliver to thee'. It is clearly an allusion to gold chains and bracelets about the neck for ornament of the body. And the Lord takes it on himself that he adorns his Bride with a profession and puts on her comely apparel. 'I decked thee also with ornaments, and put bracelets upon thy hands, and a chain on thy neck. And I put a jewel on thy forehead, and earrings in thine ears, and a beautiful crown upon thine head' (Ezekiel 16:11–12).

Christ confessed Nathaniel, 'Behold an Israelite indeed, in whom is no guile!' (John 1:47). And (Matthew 25:34): 'Come, ye blessed of my Father,' etc. That is a real owning of his own in an honourable company. Then we are to wear Christ as a garland and as a gold bracelet about our neck and on our forehead. The confessing of the name of Christ is the Bridegroom's favour that we wear in the eyes of men and angels— and therefore Paul professed the iron chain on his hand to be

Chapter 4. The qualification Christ requires of them

his glory, his glorious infirmities, and the marks of the Lord Jesus Christ that he carried about in his body. And again, Christ does confess his own before his Father and the holy angels, and points them out as his, and he in this life wears them as his Robe Royal. 'And the Gentiles shall see thy righteousness, and all kings thy glory: and thou shalt be called by a new name, which the mouth of the Lord shall name. Thou shalt also be a crown of glory in the hand of the Lord, and a royal diadem in the hand of thy God' (Isaiah 62:2–3).

5. There is a promise made of salvation to confession as well as faith (Romans 10:9), for 'if thou shalt confess with thy mouth the Lord Jesus, and shalt believe in thine heart that God hath raised him from the dead, thou shalt be saved'.

6. If Christ's name, his Truth, or any part of his Truth be called in question, this is a sanctifying of the Lord in our hearts (1 Peter 3:15)—a real sanctifying of him—when we 'be ready always to give an answer to every man that asketh you a reason of the hope that is in you with meekness and fear'. Many think it enough if the heart sanctify God, though they in the lips or the outward man confess him not. But Peter, speaking from his own experience, who denied Christ, thinks the heart sanctifies him not when we profess not with our mouth the reasons of the hope that is in us. Joseph of Arimathea came boldly and begged the body of Jesus. It was time then—the enemies were highest, Jesus was lowest, his body now being a piece of dead clay, his disciples having fled, none of them durst ask his body to bury it—Joseph did it with the boldness of faith.

Practical application

It is not enough to have a good heart to Christ, but with the mouth and outward man we must avow Christ. And now, when so many dishonour him by blasphemies and heresies, the Lord requires this of his own, a testimony to any opposed and controlled Truth of Christ. When the enemies spake against

Christ in his person, that he was not the Son of God, he is said to endure contradiction of sinners, and now when he endures such opposition again that same Truth, we are to believe it is the same suffering. And, as many through ignorance then spoke against Christ, so do many now. Not to confess Christ, as it is a denying of him before men, so is it a scandal on the gospel and puts reproach and shame on Christ, and is called a being ashamed of him before men:

(a) because men think Christ's cross and the name of disturbers of peace, of seditious men, or opposing of authority to be a reproach, and:

(b) when out of weakness, for fear of men, we deny any Truth, we think Christ weak and not able to bear us out in standing for his Truth, and cannot but be ashamed of a weak God.

Part 2: What faith it is Christ requires of them

'Believe ye that I am able to do this?' Now the question is: What faith Christ requires in these blind men, whether faith in God as Creator or in God as Mediator?

Now it appears by the text that he requires faith in himself as the Redeemer of man—for he says not, 'Believe ye that God is able by me to give you seeing eyes?' nor says he, 'Believe ye that I have this power by gift at the second hand from God? as if it were given to me and I had it not of myself,' but he asks, 'Believe ye that I am able to do this?' The apostles deny that they by their power had healed the cripple or could work any miracles, but that Christ in them wrought this (Acts 4:12–13). Neither can faith in God Creator be saving faith which Christ must require of these men. Hence these assertions:

First assertion

A natural faith to believe that there is a God (which devils have) can save no man.

Chapter 4. The qualification Christ requires of them

Firstly, for if so, a man's naturals [natural abilities] might take him to heaven; yea, so Christ should have died in vain as to the point of purchasing saving grace and the Holy Ghost.

Secondly, grace should be no dainty, if all men had grace, but grace shines with these rarities that are in no parts [abilities] or endowments of nature or common gifts.

(a) Saving grace comes from the highest good will and tenderest affection of God, from the heart of God. It is a question, if the creature can be in a higher capacity (remaining a creature) than to receive saving grace and glory, which is but the rose and bloom of grace. For it is like the man Christ, who has received a name above all names, above angels and men, and has such a load of grace and glory, that higher cannot be, he remaining man. Saving grace then must be a rare beam and an incomparable outflowing of God, when God could have no higher flower nor a more transcendent ornament to himself incarnate than grace and the perfection of grace. Now, common gifts and parts— such as strength, beauty, birth, wisdom, learning, knowledge—are not of so high a size.

(b) The Lord speaks of grace as of a favour shown to this man in order to heaven, not to that man; and it is not common to all, chosen or not chosen. But to buy the Pearl Christ is given to the wise merchant. Thousands go through and by [past] the field where the treasure is, and it is given to one of a thousand to find it. He 'hath saved us, and called us with an holy calling' (2 Timothy 1:9). 'Who loved me, and gave himself for me' (Galatians 2:20). Grace falls upon a certain 'I' amongst ten thousand, and upon the chosen of God, the selected flowers and roses of his tree love—by his grace I am what I am (1 Corinthians 15:10). A believer is a rose amongst ten thousand growing in the field with him, he has the smell of God.

(c) Saving grace makes not over to free will a power of tutory[18] for the kingdom of heaven, nor leaves the man to himself. Nay, it is not a 'may be' or a 'may not be' of salvation, for no salvation at all can stand with such a grace, and so may no quickening, no calling, no election, no justification. Now the Word of Truth says, 'He hath chosen us'—and that before the foundation of the world. It is not left to a 'may be' or 'may not be' as Arminians say: 'A man may be peremptorily and completely chosen to glory, if so be he continues to the end, and yet notwithstanding he may come short of continuing to the end, then the whole bargain is casten [annulled].' The Word says, 'He hath quickened us'—not 'He may quicken or he may not quicken.' The Word says, 'He hath saved, he hath called us'—not 'He may save, he may call.' But grace works to will and to do. Electing grace—justifying grace—is no changeling, nor a moon to grow or decrease, nor a sea to ebb or flow. Nor is Christ a changeling. He perfects the good work that he begins. He is the author and finisher of our faith. Gifts and a natural faith work on the powers of the soul, not to heat them but to do good to others, and may be abused and digged in the earth. The talent is a gift and confers a 'may be' only; grace that is saving cannot miscarry but must give the use of the talent.

(d) Saving grace, of its own nature, conduces [leads] to life eternal. God in Christ is the element of grace, and saving grace bends and moves toward the seat of the element. It comes from God and leads to God. It inclines to heal the soul. A natural faith cannot do this, for it is a gift rather than a grace: yea, a gift not wanting in the devils—they believe that there is a God, and tremble. So it is evident that

---

[18] The office of a tutor.

Chapter 4. The qualification Christ requires of them

Christ demands not of the blind men a natural faith in the omnipotence of God to restore them to their sight.

Second assertion

The faith that Christ requires as well pleasing to him is faith in the Mediator Christ.

(a) This is the faith that sees salvation in the despised and humbled Saviour. The natural faith seems more God-like in its object, but is not so in itself; and nature, it rests on God as God in his omnipotence. But saving faith apprehends both the lowest and the highest object—as God in a low man, poor, weak, dying, weeping—and God, high, victorious and conquering.

(b) This is the faith that more advances and extols God and abases man—because it looks to God made lowest but mighty to save, to God made poor but giving to the creature infinite riches. And there is nothing comes so near to the nature of grace as the borrowed righteousness of Christ, because it is Jehovah made our righteousness, and teaches us what a faith will please Christ—not a natural faith in which there is more nature and less will (and so less sanctified obedience), but a supernatural faith leads captive the will and depresses all heights. For the natural faith is in devils against their wills—as their natural knowledge of exact justice and of their own sin torments them, so does this faith, and therefore there is little obedience in it. The natural faith is in pagans, and how many satisfy themselves with the pagan-faith! As God termed his circumcised people Sodom and Gomorrah (Isaiah 1:10) and children of the Ethiopians (Amos 9:7), in that they had no more of God in them than the wild heathen, so most of professors[19] have no more in them than a natural pagan-faith because they

---

[19] People professing faith.

believe not in Christ the Mediator. We have much law-faith and little (yea, no) gospel-faith in us by nature. But this is yet further cleared in the third question.

Part 3: What influence faith has in the working of miracles

The third question is, What influence this faith has in Christ's working of a miracle? I answer:

First assertion

Often there is one faith of miracles, in the worker of the miracle, and another required by Christ of these on whom the miracle is wrought. I deny not but God wrought miracles by many who had no more but only the faith of miracles, as many prophesied in his name and in his name cast out devils (Matthew 7:22–23). But I crave leave to doubt whether all these workers of iniquity, that preached and wrought miracles in Christ's name, always had the use of the faith of miracles to believe that God in his omnipotence was able (and in his purpose and counsel was willing) to work such a miracle by them, *hic et nunc*,[20] even as unconverted preachers, by a mere excellent gift of God had a singular faculty or a gift[21] of preaching; but that they have a common faith to believe that God will, as at other times, assist them in the exercise of their gift at this time, is much to be doubted.

There is a faith of miracles that Christ requires in these on whom he wrought the miracle, but it is hard to prove that this is only a faith to believe that the Lord Jesus was able to work the miracle and not over and beside to believe that he was the Mediator of mankind, the promised Saviour of the world. I conceive the faith Christ required includes both. It would appear that Christ required saving faith of all—whether they did

---

[20] Latin: here and now.
[21] In Greek: charisma. [In original edition.]

Chapter 4. The qualification Christ requires of them

all believe is another question—for that. He says, 'Thy faith hath made thee whole, thy faith hath saved thee.' And it is not likely that Christ required any but saving faith of these on whom (or for whom) he wrought miracles (Mark 9:23–24). The father of the child possessed with a devil answers Christ with crying and tears, saying, 'Lord, I believe; help thou mine unbelief'—which is saving faith, so that the faith of miracles which Christ requires, as Mediator, is saving faith, it is the faith of the elect.

Second assertion

Hence, the second assertion. Faith works for the salvation of the saints.

And in working of miracles morally:

(a) It is a condition that the Lord ties himself to (Mark 9:23). Jesus says unto the father of the possessed child, 'If thou canst believe, all things are possible to him that believeth.' 'After that ye believed, ye were sealed with that Holy Spirit' (Ephesians 1:13).

(b) Faith works really, but in a spiritual manner. Faith lays hold on Christ's righteousness. And the just shall live by faith. By faith the walls of Jericho fell. But when it is said (Hebrews 11) the fathers by faith did so many great things, faith is not taken one and the same way.

For:

(i) Faith has one act when God does anything and another act when the believer does anything, as when it is said (Hebrews 11:33), by faith they 'stopped the mouths of lions' as Daniel did, and 'quenched the violence of fire' (verse 34) as the three children did, 'women received their dead raised to life again' (verse 35). That is, by faith they believed that God would do all these things, but

The Power of Faith and Prayer

otherwise faith was a mere patient[22] or non-agent as to any causality in these miraculous works. So we say, a man did such a business by trusting in a faithful friend who did the business when the man did nothing himself. Now, certain it is that faith has no physical influence in stopping the mouths of lions and hindering the fire to burn and raising the dead. Only omnipotence does all. And I believe only God, out of omnipotence of free grace, justifies the ungodly. Faith has no physical influence in so high a work, only it is a condition that the Lord requires.

(ii) But when it is said (Hebrews 11:7), 'By faith Noah, being warned of God ... prepared an ark to the saving of his house,' faith here has another act, even a moral and persuading influence, for because Noah believed a judgment to come on the world, which was not seen, upon this motive he was effectually persuaded to build an ark. So it is said (verse 8): 'By faith Abraham, when he was called to go out into a place which he should after receive for an inheritance, obeyed; and he went out, not knowing whither he went.' So (verses 24 and 25): 'By faith Moses ... refused to be called the son of Pharoah's daughter.' Faith has here another influence than in works only of omnipotence.

(iii) Faith acts by its light and influence of knowledge, as verse 22: 'By faith Joseph, when he died, made mention of the departing of the children of Israel.' He did thus prophesy from the prophetical light that God revealed to him.

(iv) Faith, as it has Christ for its object, is said to receive him. 'But as many as received him, to them gave he power to become the sons of God' (John 1:12). But who

---

[22] Inert or inactive thing.

Chapter 4. The qualification Christ requires of them

be these that receive him? He clearly answers that: 'even to them that believe on his name.' Now, this receiving of Christ is the specific act and essential work of faith, and it is all the acts that are in faith as it justifies; for the Lord Jesus, and the sinner in the matter of believing, come under diverse considerations, and in them, all we receive of Christ is by believing.

First, as receiving is a consenting to and an accepting of a man as a husband, and so it is an act of marrying him.

Second, as you have need of Christ in your poverty, by faith you accept of him as a Surety to pay your debts when you are broken and cannot pay them yourselves.

Third, as you are in danger to be condemned by conscience for want of one to plead your cause, you receive him as your Advocate, for we have (or possess, or enjoy) Christ as our Advocate when we sin (1 John 2:1). But this supposes the state of reconciliation, for a just advocate ought to plead for no unjust cause—or for no just person in an evil cause. What! is not sin an evil cause? It is true. But Christ pleads not to make sin no sin, but to make it no condemning sin, that the devil and conscience may not carry an ill cause against a pardoned sinner to condemn him. It is not a question of fact that Christ pleads for. He will grant that the believer has sinned. But it is a question of law, whether the believer ought, by law, to be condemned when it cannot be denied but that he has sinned. Christ pleads most justly that he ought not to be condemned, seeing his Surety was already condemned for him. When the sinner believes this, he receives Christ as his Advocate.

Fourth, as the sinner is in danger of hell, he receives Christ when he rests on him as his Rock. So the half-drowned man believes in the rock, that is above the sea and the proud waters, he receives and accepts the rock as a place of refuge. So the manslayer received and accepted of the city of refuge for his place of defence, and the chased man, pursued for his life, gets himself into the tower of a strong castle and he rests with all his heart on that castle and fort.

Fifth, as he is in danger of a sad sentence from a just Judge, he receives Christ as his righteousness. And though he be a sinner, and a lost sinner, yet he rests on a suffering Saviour and so receives Christ.

To sum up:
In the first consideration, Christ is the Husband.
In the second, Christ is the Surety, the sinner is the broken man.
In the third, Christ is the Advocate, and the believer the unjustly accused man.
In the fourth, Christ is the Rock and the Castle, the sinner the drowning and pursued man.
In the fifth, Christ is the suffering Saviour, the sinner the guilty person, yet absolved for Christ who suffered for him.
So that all the acts of faith (as it justifies) consist in receiving and embracing Christ.

Third assertion

Christ here requires faith as a preparation before he works the miracle. It is a condition of the extolling of Christ in his omnipotence and power, as Christ casts not mercies on us at random. For 'he did not many mighty works there because of their unbelief' (Matthew 13:58). Yet this is not so to be taken as if the only reason why God works not miracles now as then was because we believe not that he will work miracles, and that if we could believe, then he should work miracles. But it is because the gospel is abundantly sealed and confirmed already.

Chapter 4. The qualification Christ requires of them

Yet, if we would believe, God would do greater works for us; if we had more faith, we should see and enjoy more of God and his glory (John 11:40); we should receive spiritual favours, more than we do. Miracles in the same coin and in the kind of works of omnipotence wrought for our salvation do yet remain. We have the tried gold and the flower of all miracles if we believe.

Though God divides not the Red Sea for us, that we may go through dry, yet if we could believe and stand still in our great straits, we should see the same salvation of God. There is not an earthly Canaan promised to us now, yet if we believe, we enter into God's rest. And we have the inheritance of Emmanuel's eternal land, that flows with the consolations and visions of God. The sun stands not still now for two days in one, till we overcome our enemies as in the days of Joshua, but if we can believe, there shall be a new face of a glorious Church of Jews and Gentiles, in which the earth shall be filled with the knowledge of the Lord, as the waters cover the sea, and the moonlight of the gospel shall be as the sunlight, and the light of the sun as seven days in one.

God makes not now a dry staff to bud and waters to come out of the rock, but in regard of the light of the gospel, we have the marrow and the bloom of that wonder—for the wilderness blossoms as a wild rose. And rude [uneducated] people do so shine with the knowledge of Christ that they are like the rose of Sharon and the glory of Lebanon. The savour of the knowledge of God is sweet and delicious. We cannot now remove mountains—but if we could pray and believe, the great Antichrist and the mountains of the earth (the emperors, the kings, and the powers of the world that take part with [support] him) should be humbled into the bottom of the sea.

Christ is a great honeycomb in heaven, and as much virtue and grace come out of him as ever—yea, and more. Christ now drops down showers of honey and new wine, he rains down righteousness. Believe, and you draw grace out of him. He must, in the end of the world, flow as a river and sprinkle all the nations. It is no less sin to forget his works and his noble acts now than of old, when he wrought miracles on the earth. But as faith must act and, before God, do great works, so the works of mercy, the wonders of grace, do most deeply affect us when we find that God has already wrought them on us.

When God has wrought the deliverance of his people, brought them out of Babylon and saved them, that wonder causes them to bring forth fruit. 'And I will make them and the places round about my hill a blessing; and I will cause the shower to come down in his season; there shall be showers of blessing' (Ezekiel 34:26). And what shall follow on that? 'And the tree of the field shall yield her fruit, and the earth shall yield her increase, and they shall be safe in their land, and shall know that I am the Lord, when I have broken the bands of their yoke, and delivered them out of the hand of those that served themselves of them' (verse 27). 'And ye shall know that I am the Lord, when I have opened your graves, O my people, and brought you up out of your graves, and shall put my Spirit in you, and ye shall live' (Ezekiel 37:13–14). And therefore, though the Lord requires faith in us before he works on us, it is not that our good beginnings should work all the work or be an engaging hire to bind Christ to work works of omnipotent grace in us.

Though faith be not merit, yet it is a duty, and the only instrument and key that opens Christ and his rich treasures. We are near Christ, and he is a full cloud, with child of [laden with] showers of grace. We and our fleece are dry, we have not faith to milk showers of salvation out of Christ. Were a soul in heaven at the river of the water of life, and yet were capable of unbelief, he should wither and dry up by the roots. And were he in hell and did believe, he should draw rivers out of Christ and be satiated with the fatness of heaven. Nor is there any

Chapter 4. The qualification Christ requires of them

merit and dignity in faith to do this, but Christ's institution and blessing does all.

The first thing Christ requires is faith. You bind Christ's hands if you believe not.

(a) The first thing Christ sees is faith (Matthew 9:2). 'Jesus seeing their faith said unto the sick of the palsy; Son, be of good cheer; thy sins be forgiven thee.'

(b) That which he seeks in Israel is faith (Matthew 8:10): 'I have not found so great faith, no, not in Israel.' That which he demands here is, 'Can ye believe?' And of the blind men (John 9:35): 'Dost thou believe on the Son of God?'

(c) The first work of the Holy Ghost when he comes (John 16:8–9): 'He will reprove the world of sin.' Why? What sin? 'Because they believe not', says Christ, 'on me.'

(d) He leaves it hard on the Jews (John 8:24): 'If ye believe not that I am he, ye shall die in your sins.' Unbelief is a slighting and refusing of Christ and of heaven (John 5:40, 3:18, 36).

Faith is scarce in the earth now, yet there was never more boasting of it when all glory of new light. But faith is not a new light, but as old as since righteous Abel offered sacrifice to God. For he did it by faith (Hebrews 11:4). Faith is out of fashion, and when he comes to judge the world (because there is so much injustice in it), Christ puts a question (Luke 18:8): 'Will he find faith on the earth when he comes?' This then must be the twilight of the world's evening. Faith is effectual by love, and that is very cold on earth; the faith we have is leaves without fruit. Out of unbelief grow profaneness, atheism, injustice, oppression, while the widow's eyes fail in looking up for justice. It is a faith James cannot see (James 2:18). Show me thy faith by thy works.

(i) Christ works both the work of believing and pays the wages—and so he serves himself of his own.

(ii) There is no dignity in faith more than any other grace. Yea, there seems to be less, for it is but a poor receiving vessel—the vessel has not whereof to be proud, nor can the beggar's hand that receives gold exalt itself above the giver.

(iii) God often gives much to a poor, weak, half-dead faith—such as the removing of a mountain, which is a great work to the faith that is no better than a grain of mustard seed. And it is far from merit that the great Lord Jesus, the high and lofty One, who inhabits eternity, gifts himself to a faith that can but touch the border of his garment.

(iv) Very often, where there is no faith at all but enmity with God, he shows mercy and works for his own name. If ever we be saved, it shall be without money and without price. No merits can enter heaven, neither of men or angels, save only Christ's merits. There is a sea of grace in heaven bestowed on men and angels—not one drop of merits or hire. They are servants and sons that are in heaven, but no hirelings nor any earners of wages. You cannot make faith to trade by way of merit—there are no such tradesmen there, but all redeemed captives coming with the tear in their eye and the beggar's rags to heaven, only for God's sake, and grace is a noble holding [tenure of land].

Chapter 5

The blind men's confession of their faith

THE FIFTH ARTICLE in this text is the blind men's confession of their faith: Yea Lord, we believe. In which, observe:

1. The reflex sense and knowledge they have of their own faith.

2. The pureness and spirituality of their faith. Christ both speaks and touches their eyes—but they require neither the one nor the other, but simply profess, 'Lord, we believe'. For the manner, or condition, of way, they refer that to Christ and his wisdom: 'Yea, Lord.'

Part 1: The reflex action of their faith

Touching the first, they profess that they believe. The doctrine is: saints may be so assured that they have saving grace and faith, that they dare and may confidently say to Christ in his face, 'Lord, we have saving grace, Lord, we believe.' So the father of the dumb child (Mark 9:24): 'Lord, I believe.' So Thomas, when sense spoke Christ to him, answered and said unto him, 'My Lord and my God' (John 20:28). 'All this is come upon us; yet have we not forgotten thee, neither have we dealt falsely in thy covenant' (Psalm 44:17). 'This is our God; we have waited for him' (Isaiah 25:9).

1. Though saving grace grows as the bones of the child in the womb, and moves and blows as the wind that we know not, yet none can go to glory never seeing nor knowing whether they have saving grace or not. Thousands go to hell sleeping, and though wakened, yet not awake; not knowing their sins and the weight of wrath and guilt. But men go to heaven waking (I speak of those come to age) and knowing in some measure the weight of the grace of God. The sweet music, the fairness and loveliness of the workings of Christ, must sometime be known, and Christ makes such a sweet stirring and such a sweet and pleasant noise of a most lovely din in the soul, that it must know he is there. I grant the motions and actings of the Spirit in the soul are thin, subtle, and often we are below Christ's dispensation in the soul. The ebbings are very low, so that we cannot discern if it be Christ that walks in the soul at our first beginning. God speaks, and we think Eli, not God, speaks. Christ speaks, and we think he is the gardener (John 20:15).

2. Other times the flowings of Christ are so high, that we are drowned and over-sensed,[23] that we speak we know not what (as Luke chapter 9). Peter is half in heaven when Christ is transfigured. He is so drunken and over-filled with the joy of the vision of glory, that he would never be out of that state. But (verse 33) he spoke he knew not what.

3. We cannot, because of inadvertence and dullness, put a right sense on his irradiations and the shinings of the Spirit. Jacob sees a ladder reaching from earth to heaven, and the angels ascending and descending, but Jacob sleeps, and while he sleeps, God reveals himself to him in a glorious manner (Genesis 28:13, 15): 'I am the Lord God of Abraham. ... Behold, I

---

[23] Our senses are overwhelmed.

Chapter 5. The blind men's confession of their faith

am with thee, and will keep thee … I will not leave thee.' All this while, Jacob knows not what the matter means. But (verse 16) 'Jacob awaked out of his sleep, and he said, Surely the Lord is in this place; and I knew it not'.

4. The affections and heart will be awake to know him, and the coals of love will be burning in the heart, and the soul sleeping (Song of Solomon 5:1). The understanding will be in a cloud even when Christ knocks sweetly. Christ confers sweetly with two disciples and their heart burns within them while he talks with them (Luke 24:32). But the mind is veiled (verse 16): 'Their eyes were holden that they should not know him.' Cleopas calls him 'a stranger in Jerusalem' (verse 18).

5. We do not know what a humbling desertion after a sweet ravishment means, because we are ignorant of our corruption and pride of nature. Paul (2 Corinthians 12:1–5) is taken up to the king's high palace and sees the gospel visions of God, and immediately he is laid so low that the devil buffets him. When he prays thrice (verses 7–8) for the removal of that messenger of Satan, by the answer that God gave him—which was half a refusal, a negative of grace—'My grace is sufficient for thee' (verse 9). It is clear Paul knew not he was in danger to be puffed up because of that high revelation, until the Lord's answer taught him so much.

6. Christ shines in his beauty of glory to John, but John's fear and ignorance or forgetfulness of three points—(a) the eternity, (b) the death, (c) the victory and resurrection of Christ—confounds him so with terror that he falls down dead at Christ's feet, till Christ lays his hand on his head and preaches to him (Revelation 1:17–18): 'Fear not—misknow [ignore] not your friends, John, you mistake me—I am the First and the Last; I was dead and am alive.'

7. We can sometimes misapprehend ourselves (Jonah 2:4): 'I am cast out of thy sight'—and slander Christ (Psalm 77:9):

The Power of Faith and Prayer

'Hath God forgotten to be gracious?' This comes from some great sin or from desertion.

Part 2: The pureness and spirituality of their faith

The saints give experimental testimony of the actings of God in them, as Jacob (Genesis 49:18): 'I have waited for thy salvation, O Lord.' Hannah said (1 Samuel 2:1): 'My heart rejoiceth in the Lord, my horn is exalted in the Lord.'

Job passes this sentence of himself (Job 23:11–12): 'My foot hath held his steps, his way have I kept, and not declined. Neither have I gone back from the commandment of his lips; I have esteemed the words of his mouth more than my necessary food.'

David says (Psalm 63:8), 'My soul followeth hard after thee.' 'How sweet are thy words unto my taste! yea, sweeter than honey to my mouth!' (Psalm 119:103). 'My heart is not haughty, nor mine eyes lofty. Surely I have behaved ... myself, as a child that is weaned of his mother' (Psalm 131:1–2).

The spouse (Song of Solomon 2:3–5): 'I sat down under his shadow with great delight, and his fruit was sweet to my taste. He brought me to the banqueting house, and his banner over me was love. Stay me with flagons, comfort me with apples: for I am sick of love.' And many the like expressions are in that Song, as Song 3:1–6. And Paul says (Galatians 2:20), 'I live; yet not I, but Christ liveth in me: and the life which I now live in the flesh I live by the faith of the Son of God, who loved me, and gave himself for me'.

Sense itself often must speak, as Paul does with the saints (Romans 5:2, 5), 'We ... rejoice in hope of the glory of God. And hope maketh not ashamed; because the love of God is shed abroad in our hearts by the Holy Ghost which is given unto us.' 'For our rejoicing is this, the testimony of our conscience, that in simplicity and godly sincerity, not with fleshly wisdom,

Chapter 5. The blind men's confession of their faith

but by the grace of God, we have had our conversation in the world' (2 Corinthians 1:12).

Papists err, who say it is pride to any to say that they know and are persuaded they are in the state of grace, and that it is humility to doubt; that all we can say is with fear of the worst, or some conjectures, or some probabilities, or good appearances that it is well with us. But firstly, the Spirit of God is a spirit of humility (1 Corinthians 2:12): 'Now we have received, not the spirit of the world, but the spirit which is of God; that we might know the things that are freely given to us of God.' Secondly, the Spirit of God's testimony is no conjecture nor any probable fancy that may as haply be false as true. No, 'the Spirit itself beareth witness with our spirit, that we are the children of God' (Romans 8:16). This is a testimony of our state and heirship, not only of our bare actions. Nor was Paul on his topics[24] when he said (verses 38 and 39), 'For I am persuaded, that neither death, nor life, nor angels, nor principalities, nor powers, nor things present, nor things to come, nor height, nor depth, nor any other creature, shall be able to separate us from the love of God, which is in Christ Jesus our Lord'. Here are nails fastened in a sure place. Christ the Master of the assembly drives in the nails—here a triumph of faith, a sure persuasion.

But that which renders this knowledge to natural men doubtful and impossible is:

(a) It is supernatural. Reflex knowledge seems somewhat higher and subtler than direct knowledge; it is above sense. Beasts live, but they have no reflex knowledge that they live; they see and hear, but they scarcely know that they see and hear, they have no sense of the grass or fodder they did eat the last year. Men endued with reason know that they know; and because it is a work of the Spirit to believe and

---

[24] Rhetorical arguments or considerations.

a high and supernatural state and condition to be the heirs of heaven, therefore it is the work of the same Spirit to believe, and to know that we believe, or to believe that a year ago I believed and was in Christ. Natural men have neither the direct nor the reflecting light of the Spirit, because they do not have the Spirit at all.

(b) Sadducees may deny the resurrection, but after Christ raised Lazarus out of the grave, Lazarus can hardly deny it. He had experience of Christ's power in raising the dead: natural men know neither the Spirit nor his work.

(c) It is kindly [natural] to natural men to doubt of works of grace. All of us by nature have a prejudice against Christ. There is that much policy of wickedness in our nature that we are born with a slander in our heart against a Saviour. When we have done a great injury to a man, we keep still an ill mind that we have so deserved, and also that he will not forgive—an anti-gospel is in our heart by nature, that sin is good and right, that God will not give a Saviour to deliver us from sin. Sure we do more naturally believe law-justice than gospel-mercy in God incarnate, though in the general we can presume kindly. And it is usual for the children of God (either under a temptation, or when the wind of the Spirit blows not) to doubt if Christ be acting in them, or has ever acted in them, because sense of graces working is supernatural, and many times the strongest of saints will be at a stand and say, 'I am cut off from before thine eyes,' as David did (Psalm 31:22) and Jonah (Jonah 2:4) and the afflicted soul (Psalm 77:9), 'Hath God forgotten to be gracious? hath he in anger shut up his tender mercies?' For, as strongest love in us, now in a sinful condition, has a disease of jealousy following it when we misapprehend God's love, so has faith the disease of doubting when we take up erroneous opinions of omnipotence and of free grace.

Chapter 5. The blind men's confession of their faith

(d) Sense of grace and experience of bypast [past] breathings of the Holy Ghost is not always in action. It is oft overclouded and asleep, and another contrary sense comes in its place. Firstly, because we have not dominion over the actings of the Spirit—God blows in this wind with greater sovereignty than in any natural wind. Secondly, the fairest flower in a storm will lour and cast a bloom.[25] Sense of Christ has its ill hour and has not always its sharpness and edge, because it is the flower of heaven on earth and the actual sucking of honey out of the rock.

(e) The sense of grace is the white stone with the new name on it, that no man knows but he that receives it (Revelation 2:17)—even hidden from the eyes of him that receives it. And the Spirit's seal of secrecy (Ephesians 1:13 and 4:3) that closes [encloses] in a love letter the Bridegroom's bracelet and ring, his secrets and mysteries, so as a saint is hid from himself. There is a treasure and hid fountain within the soul, but he cannot feel it. This refutes also the Antinomian who will have the broad seal of the Spirit's testimony so clear and evident that the saints are never to doubt again, never to be sad again, but to feast on joy actually and on feeling of the rays and beams of the warm Sun of Righteousness ever while [constantly until] they be in heaven. But Peter says we may now be in heaviness for a season, if need be (1 Peter 1:6) and yet greatly rejoice. But not at one and the same time. They (the Antinomians) are not acquaint with the variations, the ebbings and flowings of God: this you may read in Solomon's Song, especially chapter 3 and chapter 5. There is a time when Christ is behind the wall and looks through the grates [lattice, Song 2:9]; and there is a time when he comes to his garden to feast upon the honeycomb and his spiced wine, and then the spouse has a rich feast of love and of the dainties of

---

[25] Wither and discard a bloom.

The Power of Faith and Prayer

heaven, and is taken into the king's house of wine and Christ's banner over her is love (Song 2:4), and his left hand is under her head, and his right hand doth embrace her (Song 2:6). And there is a time of swooning and lovesickness and anxious questions: 'Watchmen, saw ye him whom my soul loveth?' (Song 3:3). The manifestations of God have a winter.

Answers to some objections

Objection 1: It is a work of the spirit of bondage to doubt and argues the party to be under the law.

Answer: The consequence is naught. Every act of the spirit of bondage does not argue the reign and full dominion of the spirit of the law and of bondage—as every glance of the old lovers does not conclude a divorce of marriage between the soul and Christ.

Objection 2: But being once in Christ, we are no more under the law (or the spirit of bondage for the breach of the law) than a woman is under the government and power of a husband that is dead (Romans 7).

Answer: Every comparison halts on some foot. We are no more under the curse of the law *de jure*[26] than the wife is under subjection to the dead husband. But the question now is: If through the corruption of nature, the spirit of bondage shall break through one of its own law-bounds to the fields of the gospel and tempt a believer with legal terrors to fear the curse of the law, if the soul be therefore under the law? By no means, no more than a redeemed and justified soul is under the law because he breaks the law and sins. Antinomians may as well from this conclude that the believer, if he sins, he is under the law and a covenant of works; because sure, if anything the wife

---

[26] Latin: by right.

Chapter 5. The blind men's confession of their faith

does when the husband is dead be a failzing[27] against the conjugal duty that she owed to him—we must say the dead husband is yet a husband and she is yet under his power.

Objection 3: But the Lord ought not to usurp any dominion at all, less or more, over the believer that is dead to the law. And, therefore, any act of the law, as the law, argues the party to be under the law and not under grace.

Answer. Where is there warrant that the law ought to usurp no power at all over a believer? I conceive that the law is not dead to a believer, nor does the Holy Ghost speak so. Paul says, 'We are dead to the law,' in regard that we are dead to the condemning power and just rigour of the law, but he never said the law was dead to us. As the law is a pedagogue to lead us to Christ, and the law serves to discover sin and to humble, so because we come not perfectly to Christ in this life (and there is ever a distance, less or more, between us and Christ) and we sin daily—and if we say (even after we are justified and have come to Christ) that we have no sin, we lie: therefore the law serves to pursue, chase and humble us all our life, so long as we sin—and the date of sin's indwelling is as long as we live. Therefore, though we be dead to the law (as touching its justifying and condemning) so soon as we believe and are justified by grace, yet we have not so fully parted with the law as the dead husband has parted with the wife—because, while we live, the law is at our heels and on the chase to humble and awe us in regard of new sins and new pleas with the law to force us to flee closer and more entirely unto Christ. And in respect of the act of humiliation and renewing the faith of remission of sins in Christ's blood, we have good use of the law, as long as we break the law — which is all our life, in one measure or other.

---

[27] Failing, non-performance of an obligation.

Practical application

We would be assured of good news, but are too slack in labouring after the assured persuasion of remission, the best tidings that ever came from heaven to our ears. We would have nine charters for one inheritance, we cannot have words too many, nor writes[28] nor seals, nor confirmation sufficient of our earthly holdings. All lawyers are advised there, to make the land sure to us and ours, but slight and poor securities for our estate of grace and our being in Christ satisfy us. We slight ordinances, promises, seals and sacraments. Yet, if our spiritual state be loose, what is sure to us? We love not to be sure in our conscience, though every man would have the thing sure in itself—even a Balaam would have the end of the just sure in itself—but he will not make it sure for his own soul by working out his salvation in fear and trembling.

They said unto him, 'Yea, Lord.' The faith that the blind men profess is a recumbence on the omnipotence of Christ only. They say not as the leper (Matthew 8:2), 'If thou wilt, Lord, thou canst open our eyes,' or, 'If thou touch them and pray.' But as Christ's question was touching a simple believing the omnipotence of Christ to cure them, so they answer Christ. Hence that is the purest and soundest faith, that relies on God's omnipotence and free grace without eyeing condition, reason, creatures or means.

Hence, for the nature of a sound faith, I assert:

First assertion

Faith that is bottomed on least reason, and yet staggers not, is the soundest faith. As when we have least natural reason to bottom faith, then to believe is sound faith, as Isaiah 8:17. There are ill appearances and wicked confederacies. Yet the prophet says, 'I will wait upon the Lord that hideth his face

---

[28] Written records or documents of a transaction.

Chapter 5. The blind men's confession of their faith

from the house of Jacob, and I will look for him.' The great fishes were devouring the little, Babylon swallowed down the kingdom of Judah, and the vision tarried, the people were not delivered (Habakkuk chapter 1). Yet the faith of the prophet goes to the watch tower and there it waits on, and the Holy Ghost commends that faith (Habakkuk 2:4): 'The just shall live by his faith.' In a time of dying, faith keeps the man alive. Abraham against hope believed in hope (Romans 4:18). Here were bad appearances: Abraham was old, Sarah's womb was dead as a grave and withered. But Abraham staggered not, he was not thrown off his feet, but stood it out (verse 21)—he was fully 'persuaded that, what he had promised, he was able also to perform'. He that believes, because reason and appearances say, 'It shall be,' believes reason rather than God.

Second assertion

That is the soundest faith, that sets before God fewest ways and means, and gives widest bounds to great omnipotence, as the centurion (Matthew 8:8): 'Lord, ... but speak the word only, and my servant shall be healed.' And the woman of Canaan saw no means, but much anger, wrath, sad refusals and heavy reproaches; yet she still believes and prescribes nothing to Christ; he (Isaiah 50:10) 'that walketh in darkness'—if it were twilight darkness, and had some mixture of daylight, it were good—but 'he that hath no light, let him trust in the name of the Lord, and stay upon his God'. When the Red Sea is before Israel, and death behind them at their heels, and mountains on every side, reason would say, 'What will God do next? God can do no more.' But Moses says (Exodus 14:13), 'Stand still, and see the salvation of the Lord, which he will show to you today.' 'Stand still' says that the people were running away from God through unbelief, as if God could do no more for them.

'See the salvation of the Lord.' How could they see salvation? It was very invisible to them. They thought they saw destruction and did choose graves in Egypt rather than the salvation they could see. Where was the salvation? It was in the bosom of omnipotence. The Lord shall fight for you.

Third assertion

That is the surest faith and most abiding that has pure God in Christ and naked omnipotence and infinite mercy for its formal object—not God as clothed with means, creatures and such second causes as he works by.

(a) Because God in Christ the Mediator is the only stay and can bear the stress and weight of the soul, and 'cursed be the man that trusteth in man, and maketh flesh his arm' (Jeremiah 17:5). 'Whosoever liveth and believeth in me shall never die' (John 11:26). 'Ye believe in God, believe also in me' (John 14:1). And Sarah by faith conceived a child when her womb was dead, because of the faithfulness of God alone. 'She judged him faithful who had promised' (Hebrews 11:11). Why? Is it such a sin to trust in man? Yea, it is, for the following words expound it: 'Whose heart departeth from the Lord.' It is no less than idolatry to trust in man as in a Saviour, as the people did who would make covenants with Egypt and Assyria to protect them against Babylon, whereas the Lord was in special covenant with Israel, as their king and their God, to defend them against these nations, and particularly discharged any such covenant.

(b) The formal object is the native and kindly object, and proves the act, of faculty, or habit. God, as God in Christ, is the object of faith, the *formale objectum quod*.[29] He that trusts in his friend for gold does formally trust in the gold, not in the friend. He that loves his wife as a whore, loves not his wife—he may be a hater of his wife notwithstanding

---

[29] A scholastic Latin phrase, signifying the formal object of faith.

Chapter 5. The blind men's confession of their faith

of that love. So he that believes in God because second causes and creatures are visibly in God's hand, believes in the means and trusts in them, not in God.

(c) To trust in God is to rest on him and to acknowledge that the only glory of both the power and the efficacy of working in the creature is in God, as if the means were dead, powerless and nothing, as 1 Corinthians 3:7: 'Neither is he that planteth any thing, neither he that watereth; but God that giveth the increase.' We trust not in Paul or Apollos as the fathers of our second birth, in the efficacy of it, but the glory of power and efficacy in them we give to God only; then we trust not in them, but in God. So Abraham believed he should have a son and gave the glory to God, and looked not to his own withered body nor to Sarah's dead womb, but looked to God as the only Father as if father and mother had been dead.

(d) That is the excellent mine of gold where there is least ore and most of the pure metal. The more of the Spirit there is in faith, the more spiritual it is—it is the finer gold—as when naked omnipotence and only God is looked to. Jehoshaphat (2 Chronicles 20:12) in a great strait: 'We have no might against this great company that cometh against us; neither know we what to do: but our eyes are upon thee.'

(e) When all fail us but God (as Job 19:25), yet believe through a cloud.

(f) When corruption speaks positively against omnipotence, then must Martha believe (John 11:39–40). And when the fig tree blossoms not (Habakkuk 3.17–19), yet 'the Lord God is my strength'. That is a spiritual faith. Hence by the way, we may trust men as instruments under God, as these by whom God works our deliverance and help, and not be guilty of idolatry if we trust not in them nor advance them to the chair of God. So may we love men, praise men, use second causes as God's instruments, and they may have of us love, fear, reverence, confidence, hope, without any impeachment of the glory of omnipotence, because God works our deliverance and comfort by the creatures. And God is willing that they be acknowledged in their place. And the like I say of ordinances, word and seals. But for the act of adoration (either internal, such as is the recognition and acknowledgement of God's supremacy; or external religious knee-bowing, or praying to, or religious praising or glorifying the creature, men or angels), God will have no creatures to be his under factors [agents] or deputies. Adoration is essentially an extolling and heightening of God as God, as the first efficient and last end of all things, and he will divide this with no creature. So religious faith, or fear, or hope, is due to no creature.

Practical applications

1. Hence we are taught to use means, but still to trust in God. Nevertheless, we oft believe God can feed us.

(a) When the wine-press bursts with new wine, and the girnels [storehouses] and barns are full, and the table fat, and the cup runs over, we believe God can heal us when the disease is ordinary and the physician is skilled. I doubt not but Asa trusted for health from the Lord, but the text says, 'He sought not to the Lord, but to the physicians' (2 Chronicles 16:12). When we have a strong multitude, we believe we shall have the victory. Our hearts are most whorish and idolatrous. Seldom see we both God and the creature work together but we give out a whore's heart-look on the creature, as if the Creator were nothing and the creature were all. In using means, as if means could do it, we are not half careful in fearing lest God bless not the means. We are too distrustful, as if God cared no more for his own glory,

Chapter 5. The blind men's confession of their faith

covenant, and cause than we do, or as if God had not a greater love to the Spouse of Christ than we: so we usurp the Bridegroom's love and care and fill not our own chair in the use of means.

(b) The largest and weightiest side of our faith, when we trust in God, is bottomed on second causes. Hence comes a secret kissing of our own hand. It is much to look to the sun and acknowledge it to be a candle in God's hand; many have adored the sun as God.

(c) But when the creature is ourself and there is an eminence in ourselves, our own wisdom, virtue, goodness and learning court and favour princes and strength. We are more glorious than sun or moon, or all the heavens and stars, and there is not a greater God than 'self' or 'I' in heaven and earth, because self-love promoves [fosters] idolatry—as one sin flatters and serves slavishly another, as if when God created 'self' he had made a greater, a fairer and more eminent God than himself. When in the meantime it is impossible that God can make a God like himself, or that anything that he had created can amount to any higher than a shadow. Angels, or angels in millions of degrees above the angels that now are, could be nothing but shadows of God, and poor, fair beautiful nothings. God can (and has) begotten one Son, his substantial Self, but it involves an eternal contradiction, though God should soder [solder] and melt in one all the perfections of angels, that one angel should be so, so far elevated above the poor mother nothing (which is the only necessary and essential seed of all creatures) as that it could rise higher than to be an excellent rational shadow of an intellectual and shining nothing that can be (and certainly is) annihilated and may be turned to nothing by omnipotence that made it out of nothing.

The Power of Faith and Prayer

2. It is only faith, for the soul to cast itself on omnipotence. All created beings are just nothing, and the faith of saints can be bottomed and rest on nothing but God only. Only omnipotence can go between the sinner and eternal wrath, and between the being of a saint and eternal nothing, for providence has so disposed—and otherwise it cannot be—that there is a weakness in every creature to interpose itself between pure nothing and its fellow creature, because it is itself originally nothing and so cannot give it to its fellow creature what it has not in and from itself. And therefore God only can sustain the falling creature, and if the creature trusts in a fellow creature, it is but an empty thing, a weak reed, and cannot bear up the weight of the faith of the intellectual creature. Trust in the Lord and 'let Israel hope in the Lord; for with the Lord there is mercy, and with him is plenteous redemption' (Psalm 130:7).

When all means fail and dry up, faith casts itself upon omnipotence—it is a strong pillar. I am undone, but God can help. It is true, faith rests on God in the use of means, but not for the use of means or because of means. Believe that God feeds you by bread, but believe it not that for bread he can do it. Believe that God saves by an army, but not for an army. Yea, rest on him that justifies the ungodly, believer, for free grace, but not for believing. It is much to know the formal object of faith and to trust God for food when there is no bread, and for deliverance when the enemy is strong and we weak. Faith is to set God on work as God and as pure, naked, only omnipotence when we look on creatures and means as mere accidents [fortuitous occurrences] to omnipotence—they are neither up nor down to God, and faith looks at them as mere indifferences [unimportant matters] to God: he can save with few or many, he can feed us with bread or no bread. We are tied to means as duties. God and omnipotence are above means. God, as God alone without any fellow God, 'bringeth down to the grave, and bringeth up' (1 Samuel 2:6).

Chapter 6

The cure

THEN TOUCHED HE THEIR EYES, saying, According to your faith be it unto you (Matthew 9:29).

Part 1: Christ's action

In the manner of the cure there are two things—a sign and a word of omnipotence. 'Then touched he their eyes.' Christ might have healed with a word, but he adds a sign—he lays his holy hand on the eyes of the blind men. He does this to testify that Christ's bowels pitied both the bodily misery of blind eyes in the men, and to strengthen their weak faith. See hence, how far the indulgence and compassion of the Mediator Christ extends to our misery, spiritual or bodily—these may give light.

First assertion

Christ sundry times in the manner of his miraculous curing condescends to signs of great indulgence.

1. He condescends, coming to the sick and diseased, as he came to the graveside of Lazarus, to the coffin of Jairus' daughter. We know his sweet words of condescension to the centurion for his servant: 'I will come and heal him' (Matthew 8:7). He came to the man that lay thirty-eight years at the pool.

He came to his own (John 1:12). He came 'to seek and to save that which was lost' (Luke 19:10). 'My Father' and I 'will come unto him, and make our abode with him' (John 14:23). It was beyond our deservings that he should receive and welcome the diseased and the lost sinner, but that Christ should be at pains to come to his enemies is humble condescension of love. He comes near our spiritual diseases, to handle and feel our wounds. 'I said unto thee, Live' (Ezekiel 16:6). I looked on thee, my heart came up to my two eyes in that love-look (verse 8) and 'I spread my skirt over thee'.

2. Besides coming, there is touching of our boils and sores. His hands touched the defiled skin of the leper, and he puts his fingers on the eye-holes of the blind, makes clay and spittle and salve, and anoints the eyes of a man born blind (John 9:11). He touched the hand of Peter's mother-in-law 'and the fever left her' (Matthew 8:15).

3. He so pained [exerted] himself to cure all manner of diseases, that he is said to take a lift of [to carry] our diseases and to bear them (Matthew 8:17).

4. He seeks us—we seek not him (Luke 19:10). The lost sheep has more need of the shepherd than the shepherd has of it. Yet, as if we were worthy of the seeking (Luke 15:1 4), he leaves the ninety-nine in the wilderness to seek us.

5. It is much condescension of love that he took on him man's nature to suffer a pained and broken body, and hunger, thirst, weariness, cold, death, heaviness of soul, fear, grief and weeping, which are infirmities of the same kind and nature with our bodily and soul weaknesses. So as Christ would lie sick in the same sick-bed with his friends, he would extend his humane bowels of compassion and man's mercy to the leper (Mark 1:41), and sigh with a man's heart and weep with a man's eyes for the sinners in Jerusalem and bemoan them (Luke 19:41–42; Matthew 23:37–38).

Second assertion

Christ pities weak faith, so far as to bind up the broken reed and to cherish the fire and light of a smoking flax. He shall not cry (Isaiah 42:2). He shall speak sweetly and calmly beneath his voice, he shall not 'lift up, nor cause his voice to be heard in the street'. He is not skilled in scolding and shouting. And to carry the lambs in his bosom, a place near to his bowels and heart, he drives gently those that are with young (Isaiah 40:11). We are short-breathed in our way.

Third assertion

Sin, as sin, does not actually move Christ to pity, for then he should pity all sin, even of devils and against the Holy Ghost and final impenitence, which are the greatest sins. It would appear that misery in the creature is the object of God's compassion, but then his compassion is not an inclination loosed from freedom and liberty of free will, but it is the actual exercise of mercy tempered with wisdom, liberty and justice. Hence God decreed freely never to show mercy on sins committed with the highest hand.

Then the gentleness and mercy of Christ God, and all the affections of God, have his infinite understanding, infinite wisdom, freedom, sovereignty and justice (as it were) diffused through them in the actual exercise of them toward objects without [external to] him. Our affections have not liberty, reason, discourse [freedom] actually to temper them, but run upon wheels of natural affection (almost as the elements move—as light bodies ascend and weighty bodies descend), especially in their first rise [beginning].

Practical applications

1. The first use is a commendation of the gentleness and meekness of Christ, who does so humble his sweet compassionating nature as to touch our botches [sores] and natural defilements.

He that will touch blind eyes has compassion on the miseries of his saints. What! do we not in our thoughts accuse the Lord of cruelty, that he lays Germany waste, has made a garden of God a den of dragons, turned Ireland into a wilderness and a land of drought, and hewn down so many with the pestilence and the sword of a stranger, and the civil sword in Scotland, that the land is unpeopled, the living being unable to dig graves for the dead? Yet has Christ the bowels of God and infinite mercy. He knows wherefore all this is—justice cannot overtop [surpass] infinite mercy. There cannot be such a God as we serve, so gentle, tender, meek, indulgent, whatever contrary thoughts we have of him in the ague of our intemperate heart-risings in our sufferings.

2. If Christ pities blind eyes, he also pities a blind heart and all the corruptions of our nature, and his mercy is the more tender that he sees us wrestling with unbelief and burdened, pained and overwhelmed in spirit, with a hard heart. Could we lay our spiritual wounds before Christ, he that touched the blind eyes out of tender compassion can touch a blind heart and loose an obdured [impenitent, stubborn] soul out of its fetters (Jeremiah 3:22). 'That thou mayest say to the prisoners, Go forth' (Isaiah 49:9).

But is that enough to say? Yea, it is. His word can break through iron chains. And if this were not enough, he is anointed 'to preach good tidings to the meek' (Isaiah 61:9)— and there is more than words—'He hath sent me to bind up the brokenhearted'—this is an almsdeed and not a word only. But we do not employ him. We might be afraid, if we thought Christ to be changed and that he were not the old Saviour, but he has the same heart and infinite compassion in heaven that he had in the days of his flesh.

3. We would [ought to] beware of sinning presumptuously and with a high hand. Such sins in a manner, or in respect of God's decree, overcome the mercy and gentleness of Christ, in regard

that he has decreed to deny mercy to final obstinacy. Frequent sins against the sparks of divine enlightenings in an illuminated conscience border upon an affront and an indignity done to mercy. It is one thing to sin against mercy—all our sins offend against mercy—but to reproach mercy is another thing. It is a dangerous sin and borders well near upon hell. God, by his decree revealed in his word, has put a special hell-mark upon sins of obstinacy, and sinning against the Holy Ghost, and with a high and lifted-up hand. The decree of God has lifted those sins beyond the lines of mercy. It is safe in no sort to sin, but it is terrible to sin on the other side of pardoning mercy. It is less dangerous to sin on this side of free grace; if you overpass the bounds of rich grace in sinning, you have done with it [finished with it].

Part 2: Christ's words

In this cure, besides the sign, Christ speaks words to the blind men for the strengthening of their faith; whereas without signs or touching or words, he could have opened their eyes. 'According to your faith be it unto you' is: 'If you believe, the deed is done. If not, ye are yet blind.' Hence it is a question, if the measure of our believing be a rule and measure to God in giving grace and working deliverance.

First assertion

The only determining and binding rule that the Lord walks by in showing mercy on us, is the free grace of God. 'But Hazael king of Syria oppressed Israel all the days of Jehoahaz. And the Lord was gracious unto them, and had compassion on them, and had respect unto them, because of his covenant with Abraham, Isaac, and Jacob, and would not destroy them, neither cast he them from his presence as yet' (2 Kings 13:22–23). 'The children rebelled against me: ... then I said, I would pour out my fury upon them, to accomplish my anger against them in the wilderness. Nevertheless I withdrew mine hand,

and wrought for my name's sake, that it should not be polluted in the sight of the heathen' (Ezekiel 20:21–22). 'Therefore say unto the house of Israel, Thus saith the Lord God, I do not this for your sakes, O house of Israel, but for mine holy name's sake, which ye have profaned among the heathen, whither they went' (Ezekiel 36:22). And he gives the reason why he removes the heart of stone and gives a new heart to them (verse 32): 'Not for your sakes do I this, saith the Lord God, be it known unto you.' Why! were they not a holy people? No! 'Be ashamed and confounded for your own ways, O house of Israel.' Grace is a noble principle, and God regulates himself in his dispensations towards us, to walk with his elect according to the principles of free grace.

Second assertion

Faith is a made rule, by God's appointment and free decree, not of its own nature, according to which the Lord walks. So God justifies the ungodly, if he believes. 'He that believeth on the Son hath everlasting life' (John 3:36). 'If ye be willing and obedient, ye shall eat the good of the land' (Isaiah 1:19).

Third assertion

Often the Lord is pleased to accommodate the measure of his gracious working, according to the measure of our faith, as the centurion's strong faith receives a present [immediate] healing of his servant without more ado. 'Open thy mouth wide, and I will fill it' (Psalm 81:10). As wide as the vessel is, so large is the Lord in pouring in mercy. Oh! how narrow are we? What an incapacity to receive God—like a circle a thousand times less than that of the earth, that cannot contain within its sides a circle of the quantity of a thousand earths!

Chapter 6. The cure

Fourth assertion

Our faith is not a measuring rule, leading and circumscribing the Lord in all his ways and acts of free grace to us.

(a) Because God gives a new heart and a new spirit; and so faith itself, where there is no faith at all, as being found of them that never sought him (Isaiah 65:1). All grace (and thus faith) is like a precious pearl, of exceeding great worth, that a poor man finds in a waste wilderness by chance and mere hazard, when he never thought of it. Just as Saul seeks his father's asses, and he finds a kingdom ere he comes home, Christ comes on a man with the jewel of faith, ere ever he be aware or know what he is doing. The beginning of the kingdom of heaven is mere lottery[30] to the soul that finds it Ephesians 1:11). Believing is a sudden bargain. Men are not put to any saving deliberation, 'Shall I take Christ, or shall I forbear?' Christ wins a consent without a consent; he makes the marriage himself alone, for no man can savingly intend to believe before he believes. Christ is within doors first, and then you give a saving consent to open to him. Christ is not welcomed before he comes.

(b) There is nothing without God that can limit acts of omnipotent grace. Though you had a mind to sail to heaven, yet you cannot buy a wind. The workings of the Holy Spirit are like the blowings of the wind. The husbandman, when clouds refuse rain, by industry can make a sort of rain and water his garden, but neither can the husbandman nor the sailor by any art [skill] make wind. All the kings of the earth, when it is calm, cannot command the blowing of a little air of wind. When the wind is in the east, all the powers and strength of men cannot change it to the west. So the motions and blowings of the wind of the Spirit depend on the Holy Ghost only—not on our gracious acts of believing,

---

[30] Something which comes by divine providence.

because acts of believing are themselves free and independent breathings of the Holy Ghost, and one wind cannot create another. God makes all motions in the air, and omnipotence creates all gracious acts in the soul.

(c) Even after we believe, Christ gives more than faith or our desires can ask or crave (Ephesians 3:20).

(i) Therefore the measures and degrees of the motions of grace are exceedingly various in one and the same soul. There will be a strong and mighty blowing of the Holy Ghost just now, and presently [immediately] after, a slow, a lent [sluggish] and quiet breathing, as is clear in David, who had both high feast days of entire communion with God and ordinary breathings of God, as Psalm 31 and Psalm 63 compared together do clear [make clear].

(ii) Sometimes there is strong communion with God in Christ (Song 3:4): 'I held him, and would not let him go.' And sometimes so low ebbings that the spouse says (Song 5:6), 'My soul failed (Hebrew: went out of) me when he spake: I sought him, but I could not find him; I called him, but he gave me no answer.'

(iii) It is not possible, in regard of ordinary dispensation, that Moses could always be in such a rapture as to wish his name to be blotted out of the book of life for the salvation of the Israel of God. For then he could not have spoken so unadvisedly and unbelievingly at the Waters of Strife.[31] Nor can God (except he would make the way to heaven and the home all one) so order the salvation of his elect as that there shall be nothing but the sweetest manifestations of Christ all along the way to heaven.

---

[31] Waters of Meribah—see Numbers 20:13.

Chapter 6. The cure

(iv) As there are some highest manifestations of God, in which experience teaches that the saints would not be able to keep the use of a tabernacle of clay with that little heaven, so neither are the saints to make high manifestations God's constant rule. As David's soul is filled with marrow and fatness, he may desire the same again. 'My soul thirsteth for thee ... in a dry and thirsty land, where no water is; to see thy power and thy glory, so as I have seen thee in the sanctuary' (Psalm 63:1–2). 'When I remember these things, I pour out my soul in me: for I had gone with the multitude, I went with them to the house of God, with the voice of joy and praise, with a multitude that kept holy day' (Psalm 42:4). But it is a doubt, if he looked for such communion with God again until he were in heaven, or if he expected such a high spring tide of faith, with a soul enlarged to be capable of such shinings and morning dawnings of heaven's glory in this life. That would seem to be a limiting of the sovereign dispensation of grace. Again, let a believer have such a rapture as Paul had, when ravished to the third heaven, as the saints may have the like in another spiritual way, yet is he not to lay down this ground: 'Sure I shall have as high a manifestation of God, ere I die, as this was.' Are believers, when heightened above their ordinary in the visions of God here below, to conclude that they shall have as sweet and as high manifestations of God again? No, they are not, unless it were revealed that it shall be so.

(d) Hence, the measure and elevation of the Lord's sweet embracements cannot be reckoned according to the measure of our faith for the present. And whether God will reveal himself in as high a measure as ever he did (or never in so high a measure) is not to be determined either on the one side or on the other, because the Word of God is our rule. But God's dispensations of the measure of faith and manifestations—especially as they come to us in this life—are no way the rule that we should walk by.

(e) The measure and degrees of faith and saving grace are without the essence of either. They are not the fundamentals or essentials of our salvation. And therefore, seeing Christ may have his saints without the highest measure of faith, we are not to set a law to the Lord in giving but to ourselves in growing, for we are commanded to 'grow in grace, and in the knowledge of our Lord and Saviour Jesus Christ' (2 Peter 3:18). If Christ gives more than we looked for—or less—the duty of growing should take up our hearts more than the variety of God's dispensations. Some men have more bread than they (or theirs) can eat in this life, and some have less. Yet God feeds them both. Some have much saving grace, some have little. A penny candle shows the way to heaven to some, others are led to it by the daylight of a borrowed glory. However, Christ is wise enough and open-hearted in giving.

Fifth assertion

A little faith lays hold on an eternal redemption and an everlasting righteousness, as well as a strong faith.

(a) The weakest believer is justified by faith, as well as the strongest. The faith of the father of the dumb child who said (Mark 9:24), 'Lord, I believe; help thou mine unbelief,' did his business. The disciples with little faith and much doubting came to dry land (Matthew 8:23–27). A little hand with small fingers may receive a great heaven and lay hold on the great Saviour of the world.

(b) Though the Lord bestows out of free grace, yet ordinarily he never gives below the wideness and capacity of faith. A wide faith receives a rich alms. Where there is much, the Lord gives much. He delights to fill his own coffers and augment his treasures of grace. Yet, a caution is necessary here.

(i) Freedom of grace (and that without all merit) has no less place in rewarding a rich faith with riches of grace than in rewarding a weak faith.

(ii) When we will and run most, even spiritually, we do not bring home richest mercy. Early rising, night watching, even in this spiritual labouring, often has not the richest reward—because God will have free will's natural sweating cried down and grace to shine like heaven—and because we are ready to sacrifice to ourselves and not to burn incense to Christ and his free grace. Paul laboured much to gain the Jews, yet he was forced to leave them and turn to the Gentiles (Acts 13:46). Moses did and suffered more than Joshua in leading the people through the wilderness, yet Joshua led in the people to the Holy Land and possessed it with them, and Moses never set his foot in it. It is sometimes with grace as with the blessing: Esau did sweat and hunt for the blessing, yea and sought it with tears, but obtained it not; Jacob stayed at home and wept not, and yet obtained it. Often we trust to our endeavours, even of grace, but we come short of what we look for.

Sixth assertion

Often Christ does outshame [greatly shame] our unbelief and sin is an occasion of free grace. Christ causes thistles to bring forth figs and thorn trees to bear olives and winegrapes (as Ezekiel 36:23–26) because his people had profaned his name among the heathen, for that (and upon no other occasion or material cause) he promises to sprinkle them with clean water from all their idols and give them a new heart. Yea, grace triumphs so much over wilful wickedness that, because unbelieving Ahaz refuses a sign when God offers it, therefore the Lord himself will give a sign, that 'a virgin shall conceive, and bear a son' (Isaiah 7:14). Here the fairest rose that grows in God's garden, the free grace of God springs out of the earth—God takes occasion from obstinate rebellion and unbelief to exalt and magnify his rich goodness. Yea, the palace of glory, in which Psalms of glory are eternally sung to the Lamb, is reared up out of the ashes and dust of men's sins and high provocations.

Because men will be wickedly low and base in sinning, Christ will be richly and graciously high and overexalted [supremely exalted] in pardoning. Hell and sin must be a part of the tune of the new Psalm in heaven. The father of the prodigal had compassion on his son, his bowels were moved for him when he saw him (Luke 15:20). Why compassion on him? Because he was coming home and repenting? No! The object of compassion is misery. Repentance is a work of grace, not misery. He had compassion on him for his sin in running away from his father and riotous living, and the miserable state it had brought him into. Sin and misery were the material cause and only occasion of his father's compassion. All the bankrupts and broken debtors of grace cry eternally (Revelation 5:9–10), 'Thou art worthy to take the book, and to open the seals thereof: for thou wast slain, and hast redeemed us to God by thy blood out of every kindred, and tongue, and people, and nation; and hast made us unto our God kings and priests: and we shall reign on the earth.'

Practical applications

1. Faith is now out of fashion.

> (a) All men indeed say they have faith, but Christ says almost no man has it, and in the latter days faith shall scarce be found in the earth. Paul says all men have not faith.

Chapter 6. The cure

(b) New opinions go for [pass for] faith. Jude wills us to contend for faith (verse 3). Now men fight, side for and print for opinions and new ways unknown in former ages. But faith is one thing, sects and new lights another. Faith has an innocent, meek pen; the pen of men following new sides is bloody and full of gall to their brethren.

(c) Many think to come to heaven by works without faith, but without faith none can please God. All in heaven are sanctified, and sanctification is joined with belief of the Truth. The sect of Civilians[32] and moral, honest men by Christ's word shall not enter into heaven (John 3:3). The multitude looks for salvation by good meaning [intention] and good prayers, but the text refers salvation to faith and not to good meaning. As you believe, so shall it be to you when the soul goes in to the land of eternity. And so shall it be with you when Christ 'shall be revealed from heaven with his mighty angels' (2 Thessalonians 1:7). 'We have believed all our days,' say some. Answer these queries, Civilians:

(i) Had you ever a sick night, and a soul arraigned and pained for the want of Christ?

(ii) Have you closed the bargain of selling all lusts and bosom sins to buy Christ?

(iii) Do you make conscience of lying, lusting, swearing, cozening [acting deceitfully], though no eye but God's be witness to your actions? Or are you for an out side only, to please Church, street and mercat [market]? There is much street godliness now, but little inward heart work. Faith is no hypocrite, it is clean inside and outside.

---

[32] A sect which despised the righteousness of Christ and sought moral righteousness; *i.e.* justification by works.

(iv) Are you sick of love to Christ? Know you the absence of Christ to be a hell? and a high spring tide of the flowings of free love to be heaven? What think you of Christ's white and ruddy face, of his myrrh and spikenard? I hope you know who is your Lover.

(v) Are you often in heaven? Often with Christ? Or were you all your days in this side of time with the creature?

2. Let not the low and the poor, that are conscious to themselves of a weak faith say, 'Oh! I shall have no more of Christ than I have of faith, and if Christ says to thee, "Heaven be to thee, and eternal salvation according to thy faith," it would avail me nothing; for my faith is so little that it is just nothing and below my sense. If I get no more than my faith, I shall get nothing.' I answer:

(a) It shall be to you according as you believe, but your small, short hand and poor fingers of faith shall not be the measure. It is a little faith, but it is no little Christ that your faith lays hold on. Do not your two eyes, that are no bigger than two inches of glass, behold the wide capacious fields of heaven that lie betwixt the east and the west, the north and the south? Is not a man's brain contained in a poor little skull of small bounds? Yet a bit of heaven, a spiritual understanding is lodged there, that can reach sea, land, earth, air, sun, moon, stars, angels, heaven, the heaven of heavens, and God himself. So may a little faith lay hold on an everlasting righteousness.

(b) There would be ground for the doubt, if faith were your own work. To so little a thing, especially if wrought by nature, there is not so great a reward due as everlasting redemption. But when grace makes a bargain, it is an unequal covenant—conditions, promises, covenants and marriages made by free grace are all unequal. The creature gives little out, the Redeemer pays much in great [great things], and

Chapter 6. The cure

God gives exceeding much. Heaven is a huge thing; a cup of cold water to a disciple is a poor benefit—but God is a liberal rewarder, he gives a hundred for one, and life eternal (Matthew 19:28–29). Grace puts a great price, the price of millions of talents, on a single penny. A bit of clay of seven foot length, with a soul to warm that portion of dust, is married to the infinite Lord Jesus, the great Creator of the world, the Prince of angels and of the kings of the earth. But the grace of God made the unequal marriage—and the more unequal, the more grace in the match. The doing of the Father's will and our bit of love to God, our heart is a poor piece. But, oh how great a promise is made to it! 'If a man love me, he will keep my words: and my Father will love him' (John 14:23). Oh what a compensation!—infinite talents of love for an inch, a grain, the tenth part of an ounce of finite love, 'and we (the Father and I) will come unto him, and make our abode with him'.

(c) But despond not because of your weak faith. The promise is made to a weak faith, no less than to a strong faith. Were there a little and a small Christ promised to a weak faith, and a great and infinite Christ promised to a strong faith, the weak believer might smite on his thigh and wring his hands and say, 'Woe is me, for I am undone'. But the promise is made to faith, as faith, and not as great faith or as strong faith. Heaven and glory is due by promise to the child that can but creep, to Christ's sucking infants, as well as to aged men and fathers. There will be many weak citizens and many of the refuse of the flock and many tender lambs in heaven, who may thank Christ's tender bosom that did bear them as well as strong Abraham; poor, creeping Christians of England and Scotland set beside Moses, the greatest of the prophets, and David, the greatest of kingly prophets, who had a king's faith. This argues the transactions of the gospel to be of mere grace.

Answers to objections

Objection 1: If it must be to me according to my faith, what is my condition, who have no faith?—at least a thousand times I so apprehend. And this gospel comfort amounts to poor nothing because it pitches upon a condition in which free will has a hand.

Answer: Firstly, if salvation were referred to free will as the only disposer and author of our faith, your comfort should be cold and small. But now it is so in free will's disposing as Christ and free grace must dispose of all. Heaven is referred to the gentleness and meekness of Christ and to free graces, yea or nay. If salvation passes Christ's seal, it is a done business, were the will never so wickedly witty [knowing, wise] or frowardly [perversely] weak to refuse. Secondly, it (*i.e.* salvation) is not referred to the quantity and degree of our faith—though if it were, Christ is as able to work a strong faith as a weak faith in you—but to your faith, whether weak or strong.

Objection 2: But are there any conditions in the gospel? For salvation (some say) is not tied to belief, nor is faith a condition without which a man cannot be saved: all men, women and children (that is, the whole Church of God), are all saved, only and totally by the merits of Christ, whose merits are applied to us, sufficiently and effectually too, by his own assumption of our nature, by which we are incorporated in him.

Answer: But as that is a condition which is, firstly, commanded of God and, secondly, without which we come short of salvation, and all men are eternally damned; as, clearly, doing was a condition in the law (Romans 10:5). So is believing a condition, both commanded of God, and without it the wrath of God abides on men and they are condemned already. 'Believe on the Lord Jesus Christ, and

Chapter 6. The cure

thou shalt be saved' (Acts 16:31). 'If ye believe not that I am he, ye shall die in your sins' (John 8:24; see also John 3:18, 36).

(a) I grant it is not a purchasing condition to buy salvation, nor is it a price and ransom. Thus, Christ's blood is the only condition, but it is too low a word to call Christ's blood only a condition, for it is a noble, condign[33] satisfaction, a perfectly purchasing ransom. We do not set up faith as a collateral condition of salvation with Christ's death, for his death must have a higher room than all conditions in the world. Nor is it a joint cause with Christ. No created habit or act (though most supernatural) can ride up with the alone Redeemer who has trodden the winepress of the wrath of God Almighty; and of all the nations, there were not any with him. We profess Christ is alone in the way of purchase, merit and free redemption, and has no like, no fellow, no companion, no associates or fellow-redeemers, men or angels.

(b) Faith is a condition, not of law but of gospel—a begging, receiving condition, not working by merit nor personally fulfilling the law—but a gospel condition, exalting free grace and debasing man, as having written on it 'the base captive enslaved, and lost condition of a sinner' and heightening Christ's Royal Throne above law, men's works—yea, above the earning works and endeavours of the elect angels. There is not more gospel grace in any condition performable by men than in faith, because it towers up the glory of Christ above the heaven of heavens and preaches free righteousness and plenteous redemption in Christ, and lays flesh and blood in the dust, and lays as low as hell the bondage of the spirit of fear and condemnation.

---

[33] Severe and suitable.

The Power of Faith and Prayer

(c) It is wrought in a sweet and easy way, by the right arm of him that draws sinners out of the pit. Though acts of omnipotent grace (such as to believe in Christ and to hope for salvation in him alone) are difficult to nature and painful (yea, impossible), yet they are most unlike law works:

(i) Because omnipotence sweetly, connaturally [innately] and powerfully creates a heavenly propension [propensity] in the will and then draws out the consent, so the soul is not married to Christ against its will.

(ii) The Spirit sets faith a-going and makes it move sweetly on wheels oiled with the love of Christ and his apprehended beauty and fairness.

(iii) Because the omnipotence of grace working faith powerfully overawes the soul, leading the thoughts and the reason captive. And Christ works so strongly on the reasoning faculty, ravishing the understanding and the intellectuals [intellectual faculties] that all the witty reasonings are mastered, the mind is silenced and strongly drawn to apprehend Christ's beauty. So that, without a choice, the mind cannot but convincingly see that there is none so desirable, none so fair and lovely as Christ. The mind is brought to a spiritual drunkenness, a sweet fury of heavenly propension, and to conclude, 'I cannot pass by such a lover as Christ.' Again, comparing one reason with another, and considering all things, the soul is forced to see it is all reason, all light, to choose such a Saviour. A mass and sea of divine knowledge overwhelms the higher faculties, that the mind and understanding are forced to conclude: to whom can a condemned captive flee, but to a soul-blessing Redeemer, a rich Ransomer of lost sinners? Faith is evidence (Hebrews 11:1), an overarguing [overwhelmingly convincing] discourse, to evidence invisible beauty in Christ. And therefore sinners are drawn to Christ by way of teaching

Chapter 6. The cure

and a God teaching omnipotence. 'It is written in the prophets, And they shall be all taught of God. Every man therefore that hath heard, and hath learned of the Father, cometh unto me' (John 6:45). 'Drink abundantly, O beloved' (Song 5:1). 'Thy love is better than wine. … The king hath brought me into his chambers: we will be glad and rejoice in thee, we will remember thy love more than wine' (Song 1:2, 4). Wine is often stronger than reason. Christ so inebriates the soul with a high tide of a sea of love, that this condition of believing is sweetly and strongly wrought—and it is Christ's condition rather than ours.

Neither does Christ's taking on our nature imply any saving applying of Christ.

(a) His being the Son of Adam, and assuming a nature common to all men can never be accounted a saving application; else Pharaoh, Judas—these sons of perdition—and all the rest of the reprobate world should share with the saints in a saving application of Christ and his merits. Believing and holy walking, without which no man shall see God, would be but empty words. We were not to[34] regard a heaven or a hell: believe we or believe we not,[35] we are saved.

(b) All that savingly apply Christ are in him, as branches in the vine tree, and 'if any man be in Christ, he is a new creature' (2 Corinthians 5:17). Christ dwells and lives in him (Galatians 2:20; Ephesians 3:17) and he in Christ (John 15:5; 1 John 4:16). But there are many barren branches, cut out of Christ and cast into the fire of hell, many taken captive of the devil at his will.

---

[34] Would not have to.

[35] If we should believe or if we should not believe.

The Power of Faith and Prayer

3. We are to grow in faith, to open the mouth and the soul wide, that the Lord may fill it. If we had a longer measure of faith, if we did believe more, then we might be richer in grace, see greater things and have a sweeter and more comfortable living in Christ.

(a) We are narrow vessels and can contain little of the fullness of God. Christ is a sea of grace; we draw with little vessels, buckets of a very low size—and so we draw little out, and remain empty, dry and hungry. We bring rent bottles, leaky and running out souls to Christ (Hebrews 2:1). And we either take in little from the blessed fountain, or what we take in runs out. We do not grow fat, nor do we live on the marrow of our Lord's house—that makes souls fat and strong.

(b) We live uncomfortably. Our hearts are straitened through doubting and weakness of faith. We receive little of Christ. Because we are not enlarged to receive more, many live in the suburbs of grace, have a poor stock, and are from hand to mouth in grace all their days. They go to heaven with their grain of mustard seed, and see no great things. The farthest they come is to conflict with doubts all their life. The reasons of their poor growth are these:

(i) The life of faith is not so strongly rooted as it is in others. Trees planted half above the earth have little life and just as little fruit. They take as much summer sun and warmness, as much dew and rain, as other trees. But they have less sap of the earth. As corn on the house top never sees a harvest, the house top is ill [bad] ground. So there are many believers ill situated, too near the wayside of a mean stature of grace and a slow growth.

(ii) Men look to themselves and the storm, not to Christ. The disciples considered not who was in the ship with them, even he that created the sea and the winds. They looked to the strength of the storm and the weakness of

110

Chapter 6. The cure

the ship, and so remained weak in faith and fearful. Faith looking to God in Christ draws strength from Christ, as trading gains wealth and growing makes way for growing. Laodicea pores on what she had—she does not look to Christ and his white raiment and eyesalve; she does not feed on him and therefore remains poor, needy and naked. By looking to created grace and the stock within us, without looking to Christ, we deaden and dull faith. No man adds to his riches and wealth by barely telling [simply counting] his gold. None increases his flocks by numbering his sheep. Created graces may lead us to believe the fountain, but faith cannot feed or grow on them. Faith fetches its food from afar; it gathers life, growth and strength by exercising itself in frequent visions and acts of beholding Christ. 'For which cause we faint not; but though our outward man perish, yet the inward man is renewed day by day' (2 Corinthians 4:16). That is a growing every day, but how is this done? 'While we look not at the things which are seen, but at the things which are not seen' (verse 18).

(c) Humours hinder bodily growing, as all diseases do, and lusts and corruptions hinder spiritual growth. Strong tides overflowing the banks cast out sands that mar the growing of every green thing. The swelling of predominant lusts does much cross the life of faith and hinder the growth of grace. One lust of vainglory draws on an impossibility of believing. 'How can ye believe,' says Christ, 'which receive honour one of another?'—and it holds well, what is an enemy to life is an enemy to the growth of life. And so he might say, 'How can ye grow in believing?'

(d) Want of spiritual poverty hinders growing—we know not how little we have, and we come not to the waters of milk and wine (Isaiah 55:1). A sight and sense of need and want will make people go where they may be supplied. The thirsty man runs to the spring. If we knew how much we need and how useful Christ is, we would strive to add more and more out of him. The same esteem and apprehension that moves men to seek gold when they want it, moves them also to increase gold when they have it. The same appetite that stirs us up to seek food, excites us also to seek more food for the continuance of life.

4. Dream not that faith is merit, and that as much as you have of faith, you have as much of Christ by way of hire. For where the positive degree is denied, there must the comparative be denied also. If Christ gives not grace for the merit of faith, he cannot give more grace for the merit of more faith. There is no strict trafficking [trading] here—only Christ gives more of himself where there is more supernatural endeavouring after him—but not for our greater supernatural endeavours. But that men's labouring by the grace of God may not be in vain in the Lord, he is pleased to bless the use of five talents with the increase of other five, as he does the improving of two with the increase of other two, that no man might impute his losses to grace. In the meantime, he cannot endure that man should reckon with him thus, 'God owes me this of justice, he must pay me.'

We are to remember:

(a) Though evangelical promises of rewarding imperfect obedience makes the Lord a debtor, yet that obedience is not counted or imputed as debt (as doing was debt in the law)—though God must no less (in regard of his faithfulness) stand to his promise in the gospel than to his promise in the law, because debt and grace are friended [made friends] one with another here. In regard life was given in the law to obedience by law and right to life was a law conquest, and there was no more required but strict doing, and upon that only both the reward and right to the reward was

Chapter 6. The cure

given, *et possessio et ius*.[36] But in the gospel, possession of life eternal may be made to doing, but the strict right, *strictum ius ad vitam aeternam*,[37] is not made to doing even evangelically—that is the fruit of Christ's merits only. The works of Christ's free grace in us are the way to the kingdom, not the cause of reigning. Strict merit was in neither law nor gospel, but if merit be taken for debt to personal doing, without any righteousness in another, there is merit in the law dispensation but none in the gospel. Therefore a more noble price is given for right to heaven in the gospel than in the law, for in the law life is given for man's doing and for no other thing. In the gospel, life is given for God's suffering and the noble ransom of the blood of God—and for no other thing.

(b) Gifts are one thing, as the gift of preaching, prophesying, speaking with tongues—and saving grace (either in habit or acts) is another thing. Gifts are given without merit or desert, but some of them may also be acquired by pains and industry. A gift, as a gift, is not saving grace, yet the gracious exercise of gifts, from a gracious principle, is an act of saving grace (as in Peter's feeding of Christ's lambs because he loves the Lord Jesus). The act of feeding is the act of a mere gift; the feeding after such a manner (*i.e.* for Christ and out of this high principle, the love of Christ) is an act of grace. Saving grace can savingly act [perform] supernatural gifts, but gifts cannot act saving graces, so useful is saving grace for us.

5. Then the promises of the gospel, being most of them made to faith, teach no man to be lazy, but require of us the actings of faith, seeing it must be to every man according to his faith.

---

[36] Latin: both the possession and the right.
[37] Latin: the strict right to eternal life.

The Power of Faith and Prayer

We are not dead, passive instruments, but believing lies on us as we would eat the sweet fruits of the promises. There is:

(a) No receiving of Christ without faith—Christ forces not heaven upon dead men and blocks. But (John 1:12) 'as many as received him, to them gave he power to become the sons of God, even to them that believe on his name'.

(b) There is no life to these that believe not. 'He that believeth not is condemned already, because he hath not believed in the name of the only begotten Son of God' (John 3:18). It is a brutish thing to say that God carries men to heaven as blocks; that faith is no condition, no duty to which we are obliged: we might then cast off all fear of hell and care for heaven and give Christ such a lift [burden] of our salvation as to reject the use of all means and say, 'If Christ will not carry me to heaven sleeping, let him see to his own honour and the truth of his promises.' It is as if a merchant should say, 'The blessing of the Lord only makes rich. Therefore I'll never buy nor sell, nor take any journey by land or voyage by sea.' Or a husbandman should say, 'God only clothes the mountains and valleys with grass and corn and flocks. Therefore I'll hang up the plough and attend no flocks.'

God's showing mercy is not according to our running and willing, but it follows not, 'Therefore I should not run nor will.' Our obtaining of mercy depends upon our running and willing as means and duties, though not as causes acting upon or moving God. Thus the spouse's finding him whom her soul loved was according to her going through the streets and asking at the watchmen, 'Saw ye him whom my soul loveth?' and searching for him. And Mary Magdalene, her finding the Lord was according to her rising early and searching at the grave and weeping and asking for him. Our salvation depends upon our believing, but there is no merit here when all is done.

Chapter 6. The cure

They that seek wisdom may believe they shall find her, because she has said, 'Those that seek me early shall find me' (Proverbs 8:17). The midds [means] are not the end. The way to heaven is not heaven and the means are not God. Yet, what God has tied us to, that we must do—the rest is the Lord's. Upon the same ground, they despise the wisdom of God who say that heretics and false teachers are to be suffered, neither should the magistrate hinder them to subvert [from subverting] the faith of others, because God only can confound lies and errors by the power of his Truth. The faith of the elect cannot be quite subverted, let the tares grow till harvest. But if you argue from what God only can do and what he will do, then you ought not to admonish heretics contrary to Titus 3:10, nor rebuke these whose word eats as a gangrene or as a canker. Why? God only can confound the errors and lies of heretics by the power of his Truth. And if these be the chosen of God, they cannot remain finally heretics and they can as little render any of God's elect finally heretical.

Part 3: The effect of the cure

'And their eyes were opened; and Jesus straitly charged them, saying, See that no man know it. But they, when they were departed, spread abroad his fame in all that country.'

Now follows the miracle itself, in which Christ works that which none but God can work. To open the eyes of the blind is the prerogative of him that created eyes, ears and life (Psalm 146:8). Art [human skill] may do much to help sore eyes or dim eyes or to prevent blindness, but if the sight be quite gone and the nerves broken, all the art of man or angels cannot restore sight.

There is as much of omnipotence required to cure eyes perfectly blind as to create eyes of new [anew]. Hence a doctrine: The hardest things in the world are not too hard for the Lord. Omnipotence can do all things.

The Power of Faith and Prayer

God never made a creature but that when it is marred he can make it over again. He created all men, and when they are dissolved into dust, he can restore them to the very same life and the same bodies he created. Nature is his own proper handywork, and when nature is lame, he can make it perfect. When nature halts and crooks in its going,[38] he can heal and make it go straight. Christ is as good at the second as at the first creation. Oh! but he can make brave new work in an old soul! He can go further than to your bedside. He is the Physician of graves and dead men's bones. He makes an excellent second new world.

❈ ❈ ❈

The rest of this discourse cannot be found, it being above 50 years since the author died.

---

[38] When nature is cripple and turns out of the straight course.